PRAISE FOR *BECOMING THE BISON*

With writing that is authentic, poignant, and visceral, Kim Gameroz demonstrates an uncanny ability to capture this particular moment in education. Her stories reminded me of my stories, and this speaks to her ability to connect with her audience. *Becoming the BISON* doesn't just give educators hope; it shows them the way forward. I needed this book. You do too.

—**Dr. Danny Steele,** award-winning principal and author

Becoming The BISON is nothing short of pure gold: clear, relatable, and transformative! Kim's honest and playful approach identifies typical challenges teachers face and offers practical SEL solutions to decrease behavior issues, boost learning, and increase joy in teaching. That's right—joy. This book is an investment in yourself that can reap big dividends in your classroom.

—**Noel Foy,** founder of Neuro Noel Consulting and author of *15-Minute Focus*

Becoming The BISON is the battle cry educators have been waiting for. Kim reminds us that we don't survive the storms of our lives—we run into them with intention, courage, and community. This book is a powerful invitation to shed old systems, trust your inner truth, and lead in a way that is brave, grounded, and beautifully human. It's not just a guide for educators—it's a revolution for the soul.

—**Judi Holler,** *USA Today* bestselling author of *Holler at Your Dreams*

Becoming the BISON is a powerful, deeply human invitation to step into the storm with courage, clarity, and intention. Each chapter reminded me of my years witnessing Kim's emergence—the quiet stirring, breaking through, and the courageous embrace of her calling. This book doesn't just tell a story, it activates a sense for something more. It reminds educators, parents, and leaders that the BISON has been with us all along, waiting to be seen, heard, and finally unleashed. Insightful, resonant, and profoundly timely, this guide is for anyone ready to lead with purpose, take decisive action, and create real change in our schools and communities.

—**Diane Kay,** founder of Coaching Next Steps

Becoming the BISON is for EVERYONE in education. It's an authentic account of what it's like to be an educator and feel like you are drowning in the education system. Kim writes a personal account that is relatable to everyone involved in education. Kim takes an ideology that needs to be shared and packages it into a book that you can't NOT read. If you are an educator looking for your people and the next thing in education, then this is the book for you. Social-emotional learning is the only way to move education forward!

—**Jaime Rivetts, MSEd,** social-emotional specialist

Kim Gameroz offers a pedagogy of intention, and this book is a bold call to action for educators. Gameroz is calling for a revolution in how we approach teaching and learning. Through stories from her own experience, she challenges us to see that the way we feel—and the way we want to feel—in our classrooms and schools starts with our own choices and actions. Do not be mistaken: This book is not about social-emotional learning (SEL). This book *is* SEL. Within these pages, educators will find a guide for helping students learn how to "do school," as she makes visible the hidden factors present in every classroom that often cause students to struggle. Gameroz flips the script, showing how educators and the students they serve can step into their full potential and truly thrive.

—**Mitch Weathers,** founder and CEO of Organized Binder, Inc., and author of *Executive Functions for Every Classroom*

In *Becoming the BISON*, Kim Gameroz delivers exactly what educators have been desperately searching for: a practical, soul-nourishing road map for bringing genuine social-emotional learning (SEL) into our schools. This isn't another book filled with theoretical frameworks or "one-size-fits-all" curricula that gather dust on classroom shelves. Instead, Kim offers something far more valuable: a movement built on intentionality, community, and the courage to run headfirst into the challenges we face rather than away from them. Her BISON mentality transforms how we understand SEL, the way it ripples through our classrooms, and extends into every corner of our school communities.

What makes this book essential reading is Kim's unwavering commitment to meeting educators exactly where they are, exhausted and overwhelmed, and offering them not just strategies but sustainable systems rooted in human connection. This is the SEL foundation our profession has been waiting for. This amazing book acknowledges the messy reality of today's classrooms while providing the language, tools, and community support that actually work.

—**Joshua Stamper,** author, speaker, and leadership coach

This book is not just a book about social and emotional learning; I consider it to be a leadership book about empowerment and intention in schools.

—**T. J. Vari,** author and speaker

Kim explodes conventional wisdom about teaching and puts forth a more intentional approach grounded in community, one that can lift a teacher up by shifting perspectives and filling them with more agency and capacity. A teacher with a deeper toolbox—equipped with more than the classroom rubric—will impart upon our children a learning experience that will be powerful, purposeful, and remembered for years to come.

—**Jayme Neiman-Kimel, PhD,** ABPdN, board-certified clinical neuropsychologist

Becoming the BISON

Becoming the BISON

THE SOCIAL-EMOTIONAL SOLUTION EDUCATORS NEED RIGHT NOW

KIM GAMEROZ

This book is available at special discounts when purchased in quantity for educational purposes or for use as premiums, promotions, or fundraisers. For inquiries and details, contact the publisher at books@daveburgessconsulting.com.

Published by Dave Burgess Consulting, Inc.
Vancouver, WA
DaveBurgessConsulting.com

Library of Congress Control Number: 2026933506
Paperback ISBN: 978-1-968898-13-7
Ebook ISBN: 978-1-968898-14-4

Cover and interior design by Liz Schreiter
Edited and produced by Reading List Editorial
ReadingListEditorial.com

FOR MY SON, WYATT.

MAY YOU NEVER STOP
BECOMING THE BISON.

CONTENTS

FOREWORD

In a time when classrooms are overwhelmed by competing demands and exhausted educators, *Becoming the BISON* is a breath of fresh air—and, in many ways, a breath of life. Kim offers a grounded, compassionate guide that begins by acknowledging the reality of today's educational landscape and the daily challenges teachers face. Her voice shines through each page with clarity, passion, and hope.

Blending the best of psychology and education, Kim provides a straightforward, jargon-free road map that empowers teachers to not only transform their classrooms but to transform themselves. This is not a survival guide—it's an invitation to thrive. Kim gives readers permission to show up authentically, reconnect with their purpose, and rediscover joy in their work. You feel poured into as you read, and you're left with practical, actionable steps that make meaningful change feel possible.

Becoming the BISON is the kind of trusted companion you'll return to again and again—support in your pocket when you need it most. Kim's insight, honesty, and deep care for educators make this an essential resource for anyone committed to building healthy, inclusive, equitable spaces for students and themselves.

I'm a mother of two neurodivergent children—and a therapist, professor, and specialist who has worked with diverse learners, parents, and school systems—so Kim's vision speaks directly to both my personal and professional heart. The type of responsive, emotionally attuned, and truly inclusive classrooms she champions are the very environments I have spent my career advocating for. To see her offering educators a pathway toward creating these spaces is my dream come true. Her work is not only deeply needed, it is transformative and it has the potential to change the trajectory of countless students' lives.

—Dr. Jane Gordon, neuroaffirming marriage and family therapist

— INTRODUCTION —

Empowerment IS THE GOAL

There's a moment in every educator's journey, maybe even in your life right now, when everything feels like too much. The exhaustion. The overwhelm. The constant weight of responsibilities that extend far beyond the classroom. Maybe it's a spouse losing their job . . . again. Maybe it's an unexpected surgery for your child or an aging parent who suddenly needs your care. Maybe it's the pink slip and the budget cuts that you've been dreading. Maybe it's just the unrelenting chaos of daily life, both inside and outside of school, that leaves you wondering how much more you can carry.

Life doesn't pause when we step into our classrooms. It doesn't wait for us to catch our breath. And in a world that often feels out of control, it's easy to feel like we're just reacting, putting out fires, managing one crisis after another, always bracing for the next storm. But here's the truth: No matter what is happening around us, we all have the power to decide how we show up.

That's what it means to be intentional. It means recognizing that while we may not be in control of every situation, we do get to control the energy we bring into it and the action that we choose to take. We get to choose the way we move through our days, the way we lead in our classrooms, the way we respond to the people around us.

And here's the thing: People feel our intentions. Our students, our colleagues, our families. They feel whether we are present or just getting through the day. They feel whether we are reactive or steady, distant or connected. They feel whether we are leading with intention or just surviving until the next storm passes, hoping we make it through without breaking.

When we are intentional, others notice. They notice the calm in our presence. They notice the way we create safety in our classrooms. They notice how we lead, how we listen, how we show up, not just for our students but for ourselves. Intentionality is powerful. It shifts the way we, and others, experience our classrooms, our schools, our relationships, and our lives.

So, what if instead of waiting for circumstances to change, we became intentional about how we wanted to feel in all these spaces and social situations? What if we took action and did something about it? What if we made choices—small, everyday choices—that created more calm in the chaos, more connection in the discomfort, more clarity in the uncertainty? What if we led with the kind of energy we wanted reflected back to us?

This isn't about adding more to your plate. And it's not about doing more. It's simply about doing things differently. Intentionally. It's about recognizing that the way we feel in our classrooms, in our schools, and in our lives starts with us. When we choose to be intentional, we create environments where we and the people around us can grow into the best versions of ourselves and become who we were meant to become.

This book is about resilience. It's about grit. It's about feedback, not failure, and it's about understanding your purpose and mission. Transformation comes from conversations, not presentations. It comes from learning who your people are and what gifts you bring to the table. We're cultivating a community of educators who are ready to head into the storm and create a movement to empower, lead, and support teachers like they've never been supported before. This is a book about the future of education. Through a community of BISON, we'll lift our teachers up and finally give them exactly what they need to feel seen, heard, and supported right now.

My hope is that as you turn these pages, you will feel seen. Not in a surface-level, "we appreciate you" way but with deep, soul-level recognition of what it really means to be an educator today. Teaching isn't just lesson plans and standards. It's holding space for heartbreak, for big behaviors, for systems that feel broken. Teaching means still showing up anyway. You'll probably laugh with me at the absurdity of it all. You might cry a little too. Because if no one's said it lately, this job is hard. And yet, you're still here. That matters.

This book is for the teachers who stay late and care too much. For the school leaders who are doing their best without a map. For the parents who want to help but don't always know how. It's for the educators who crave connection in a field that can feel isolating. It's for the ones who are curious and open, who are ready to come together. This isn't about another checkbox PD but real transformation. It's about reaching the leaders who won't pretend problems don't exist and who want to start solving them together. Because when we stop surviving the storm alone and start running into it with a herd that's got our back, everything changes.

But before we can run into the storm, we must let go of the illusion that we have to do it all alone. We must also let go of the outdated beliefs we were handed—how schools should run, how students should behave, how success means perfection. Becoming the BISON is about choosing courage over comfort, clarity over compliance, and connection over control. It's about shedding what no longer serves us so we can step into new versions of ourselves—versions that are bold, grounded, and live each day with gratitude and collaboration.

By the end of this book, I want you to feel empowered to lead with intention, even when the system doesn't make it easy. I want you to know how to build a community around you that doesn't flinch when things get hard. I want you to believe you can flip the script on education entirely. Because the truth is that no one's coming to save us. But we don't need saving; we need each other.

The BISON revolution starts here. We're heading into the storm together because you were never meant to do this work alone.

PART I

Did You Say **BISON?**

— CHAPTER 1 —

Firefighter NO MORE

Let's start with the problem. Across our country, each school and school district has its own version of the systems meant to support students and their diverse needs. Our teachers feel like they're putting out fires all day long. Too many incredible educators, the ones who are spilling over with love, passion, and light, are second-guessing their worth and contemplating leaving the profession.

They don't feel truly supported by their school leaders and school communities. There's an absence of genuine, heart-centered trust and safety from another adult human being who can guide them along their journey. The solutions that our educators, principals, administrators, district leaders, and even consultants are offering are rarely more than Band-Aids stuck over the gaping cracks in the foundation.

But what if I said you could feel happier, more supported, and less judged in your classroom? What if you could stop feeling like a firefighter and start feeling like a teacher? What if your students could complete their tasks, come to school each day, and stay focused and (relatively) quiet so you could actually teach? Would you be excited to return to your classroom each day?

You see, in my years as an educator, I've learned how important it is to provide actual solutions to our foundational issues. These solutions aren't one-and-done trainings or short-lived professional development groups. They involve learning and implementing systems, strategies, visuals, and language that teachers can use every day so *they* can create a foundation. And what do we need to make that foundation strong? A focus on social-emotional learning (SEL). We need to create a long-lasting and sustainable culture built on safety, mental health, teacher wellness, executive functioning, family engagement, community building, and so much more.

SEL IN A BOX

Now, you may be thinking this approach sounds all fine and good, but isn't there a boxed curriculum for that? Or a one-day PD session or conference panel?

Unfortunately, that's the approach taken by far too many schools and districts. They present teachers with a seventy-page slide deck, a twenty-page handout, and no next steps or direction. And when you dangle the promise of SEL without delivering the goods, you create an entire community of educators who walk into their classrooms more frustrated, less equipped, and ready to throw in the towel.

All the exercises and definitions and scenarios you get from those slide decks may come in handy, sure. But it's not just about the tactics. It's about who you are as a teacher at your core. Your *foundation*. Because here's the deal: Our kids need us. They need us to teach them social and emotional skills, just like we needed someone to teach us how to deal with students' behaviors. We need to stop expecting kids to know what to do, just like how I've stopped expecting schools, districts, and families to know how to support their kids. We all need help. That's why I'm here for you—to *teach* you, not to *convince* you, that SEL is important. Because if you're reading this book, you probably at least have a gut feeling that these practices will make life better for you and your students. I'm here to help you find what you need, within yourself and your community, to put these ideas into action and sustain them for years and years to come.

— CHAPTER 2 —

Spreading THE LOVE

"No, that's not your job."

"Someone else can handle that."

"Now's not the time."

That's what I heard over and over again from school leaders, district staff, and even some fellow teachers. Maybe you've been shut down like this too. If you teach in one of the far too many districts where SEL is treated as a "character building" or "morning meeting" idea rather than a foundational practice, my guess is you know exactly what I'm talking about. But I didn't stop pushing. Because I knew that SEL-based practices were the ones that made me feel most empowered in my classroom—less like a firefighter and more like a teacher who could actually do her job: *teach*.

Let me back up. When I started teaching elementary school, after working for years as a dance teacher both at a local studio and a high school, I thought, "Okay, *this* is it. *This* is what I'm meant to be doing." I got to dance around my first-grade classroom, sing songs with my students, get excited about little things like making leprechaun traps for St. Patrick's Day and dressing up as an old lady for the hundredth day of school. We were a sweet little family, a real community.

But the work was hard. Assessments, deadlines, and the pressure I put on myself to perform for my principal made things difficult. Plus many of my students exhibited challenging behaviors daily. Some students were diagnosed (and even undiagnosed) with special needs, while others had home situations or a history of trauma that understandably caused them to not always fall in line.

No one had prepared me for this *real stuff.* No one talked about it when I was student teaching or working toward my credential. And the solutions offered by my principal, colleagues across the district, and specialists weren't helping. Putting kids in the hallway? Not helping. Having them go into another classroom to talk to a different teacher and listen to a five-minute lecture that's supposed to be a pep talk? Not helping. Keeping them in from recess? That'll really help. The shame will surely drag that unexpected behavior out of them. I honestly felt like I was putting out fires everywhere, all day long. Those token boards, PBIS tickets, points, clip charts, strategies, and fidget spinners were doing nothing. Nothing for me, and absolutely nothing for these children.

I was exhausted, out of ideas, and starting to question whether I was even cut out for this. I was about to hit my breaking point. I knew things had to change, but I kept feeding myself all the usual excuses we use to avoid taking action. *I have too much on my plate. I have a son who needs my attention. I have a husband who needs me. I need to balance work and my life. I need to work out more. I need to relax more. I need to do some sort of self-care.* And then it hit me. Something in me whispered, "There has to be a better way." Instead of sitting in the shit, instead of going through the motions, instead of watching the educators around me throw their hands up and walk away, I was going to head into the storm and do something about it. I wasn't sure what I was looking for, and I definitely didn't know if I was going to get the answers that I needed, but I knew I could not sit in this mess any longer.

I started out by visiting the speech and language pathologist at my school site. I thought that maybe she used some methods in her small groups that I could somehow bring into my classroom to support my students—*all* my students. I thought that since she saw a large number of my kids with special needs, there were skills I could incorporate into my teaching day to create some sort of common language. She offered to loan me some books to get me started, and I went home that night with an armful of pure gold.

Sitting at my kitchen table after dinner, I opened up volume 1 of Social Thinking's We Thinkers! series, and I couldn't put it down. I had all my flair pens out, and my hand could not, would not, write fast enough. I had drawings of ideas for posters and anchor charts I could make. I had ideas about how to control the tone and tempo of my voice, going low and slow, positioning myself lower than the kids, watching my proximity and body language. And I knew that it was going to work. I could feel it, and I wanted to do it all.

I decided that instead of expecting my students to automatically know how to work with their peers, set goals, or listen to one another, I was going to explicitly teach them how to foster strong relationships and navigate social situations.

Instead of lecturing my students after they did something inappropriate, we were going to have classroom conversations about the social-emotional chain reaction so I could help them understand how their actions affected others and the classroom community.

And instead of forcing my students to "ask three before me" when they didn't know what to do or where to go, I would teach them to "think with their eyes," to read the room, to notice what other students were doing, and to figure out the group plan so they could follow along and solve problems on their own.

My brain was going a million miles a minute. I was so excited about this new way of talking to my students in a language they could understand. The ideas were simple, easy to digest, and oh so beautiful. I could reinforce everything with picture books and anchor charts, and then I could bring it into everything we did.

Next, I picked up *The Zones of Regulation*. This foundational text taught me that instead of expecting my students to regulate their emotions on their own, I needed to spend time in class talking about feelings and the strategies they could use to support themselves. I would institute check-ins to see how we were feeling throughout the day, and we would choose strategies to support ourselves. We'd create a toolbox together and use visuals to remind ourselves of our strategies throughout the school day. And I was going to model all this work in front of them, all day, every day, throughout the entire school year.

I'm telling you, the excitement I felt about bringing these things into my classroom was incredible. And then when they started working? I could barely contain myself.

I went back hundreds of times to thank our speech and language pathologist for the books and to tell her about all the incredible things that were happening—all the changes that were occurring in my students and, even better, in *me*. I was calm. My students were taking care of each other. There was less arguing, less frustration, more support, and can you believe it, even more happiness. I mean, I'd thought we had a little family and community in my classroom before, but this was a whole different level of connection.

My kids were finally being taught the skills they needed. I was meeting them where they were at in all academic areas, and I was also giving them the strategies and tools they needed to support themselves socially and emotionally. It was magic.

NO TIME TO SHARE

So what's a girl to do? Keep it to herself? Pretend she didn't just find the thing every teacher was praying for? Let this group of students go on to the next grade and then try to teach their teachers these strategies? No. I knew I needed to get the word out *before* the school year turned over. So I went to my principal and asked if I could share some strategies with my colleagues at our next staff meeting. Want to know what the response was? "This is not the time to share."

I stared at her, stunned. *Not the time to share?* When teachers were crying in their cars before school? When hallway behaviors were out of control? When everyone was barely hanging on? Sure, it was the end of the school year and everyone was super busy. But behaviors were still happening all down the hallways. Teachers were still going home drained, depleted, and frustrated each day. And lunchtime in the staff lounge? *That* was exhausting to even be around.

So I didn't stop. I wouldn't. I couldn't. I knew that I needed to reach my peers. I had to help them *before* they got their new group of kids the following year. Therefore, I did what anyone on a mission would totally do: I emailed our district's director of education, our director of special education, and anyone working at the district office who had come in my classroom before and might give me the time of day. And I also did what any normal teacher would do, of course—cc'd my principal on all the emails. Totally fine, right? Yikes.

Now, I can't say this decision didn't bite me in the butt a little bit. It for sure did. And I'm pretty sure I was scolded by my principal. But did I get what I wanted? Yes. I had one of our teachers (who was on special assignment working at the district office) come in and observe me talking about feelings and tools with my class, and I was given thirty minutes at our final staff meeting of the school year to talk about some easy phrases and systems that my colleagues could use in their classrooms.

But my school site was only the beginning. Our amazing speech and language pathologist (who is truly one of my favorite humans on the face of the earth) and I took these systems and strategies and presented them at multiple master classes throughout the next school year. We had teachers from all across our district packed into my classroom for these after-school sessions, and guess what? The teachers in attendance were happy. They were excited. They felt supported. They found hope. And they wanted more of it.

Pretty soon it was like we were starring in our own little road show. I was getting emails from principals I'd never even met before asking me if I would come to *their* schools and work with *their* teachers. And teachers were creating. They were making visuals and activities to go along with all the things we were teaching them. There were leaders at their school sites who wanted to share all their stuff and their new knowledge with me. It was absolutely incredible. The connectedness I felt when I was working with these teachers, these leaders, these adults, was something that had been missing for me. I loved working with kids, but being able to create leaders and teachers who were focused on being the best versions of themselves *for* their students was filling me in an entirely new way. And I loved it.

That school year, I was blessed with yet another challenging group of students with lots and lots of big behaviors and special needs. I was also blessed with a student teacher. This was incredible because it gave me the opportunity to not only mold, teach, and guide a new teacher who was eager and excited, but it also gave me the time to really support the teachers at my school site. While my student teacher took over longer periods of the day, I went into classrooms, modeled our new phrases and systems, worked with groups of kids, and supported my colleagues. You could feel the climate of our school start to shift. Everyone started to speak the same language. We used key phrases to support and *teach* students the behaviors that were expected of them, and we were talking openly with our kiddos about their feelings and our own.

My colleagues with challenging groups of kids? They were getting through the day less anxious, less stressed, and more equipped than ever before. Teachers who'd been thinking about quitting the profession because of the struggles they'd been facing with certain kids were now able to support their students and themselves.

You could feel the transformation happening all across our campus. Walking through our hallways felt different. There was an energy, a sense of collective purpose that hadn't been there before. As a teacher,

I felt like I finally had the tools I'd been searching for my entire career. Instead of feeling helpless when challenging behaviors came up, I had language and strategies that actually worked. The constant knot in my stomach throughout the school day, that Sunday-night dread so many of us know too well—these things abated. I wasn't just surviving my days anymore; I was thriving. And seeing my colleagues experience that same shift, watching them rediscover their passion for teaching instead of counting down to retirement, was incredibly powerful. We weren't just changing our students' lives. We were reclaiming our own joy in the profession we'd chosen because we believed in making a difference.

But it couldn't just be *our* school that was the center for all social and emotional learning. This was needed in *all* schools. It had to be bigger. It needed to go everywhere. And to get it everywhere, *I* needed to be everywhere.

So how does one person get everywhere? I started reaching out to more people in my district. I met with our assistant superintendent one day after school to discuss what their plan was to move forward with these ideas. At the time, I couldn't believe I was actually sitting in her office and that she wanted feedback and ideas from me, Kim, the first-grade teacher, the gal who wore pineapple sunglasses and pineapple slides on her feet every Friday, who sang and danced to *Zootopia* with her students. This was incredible to me as an educator who felt this deep desire to share with her district and the world.

We decided to put out two exclusive professional learning opportunities that I would lead at the end of that school year. You know—when no one wants to learn one more thing, try one more strategy, or add anything else to their plate! But I had a feeling people would come. I had started my Instagram account, @SELebrateGoodTimes, where I was documenting all the systems and successes from my classroom. And I knew these educators weren't just showing up for *me*; they were showing up for themselves.

And the trainings? They were a hit! I introduced two simple systems that teachers could implement right away. They laughed, some cried, and I left those sessions feeling like I was walking on air. The message was clear: Our teachers were hungry for support. They were craving connection. They needed to feel seen. And more than anything, they needed tools that worked with their students, not against them. I left knowing I had to do more of this. Not for me. For them.

At first, I didn't even have a name for what I was doing. I just knew it was working. I thought I was just teaching systems. Just offering classroom supports and creating a common language. I didn't have fancy words for it. I didn't call it social-emotional learning. Honestly, I didn't even know what SEL was at the time. But now I can see it so clearly. That's exactly what I was doing from the beginning. Before SEL became a buzzword, I was helping students build the skills they needed to succeed not just academically but as humans navigating life. Social-emotional learning became the very foundation for everything that came next.

So what is social-emotional learning?

At its core, SEL is about helping people understand how to navigate the social world. That means teaching kids (and adults) how to manage their emotions, read a room, understand someone else's perspective, and respond in ways that build connection instead of breaking it. It's about emotional intelligence, emotional regulation, and awareness that our actions impact how others feel and how they respond to us.

It's also about executive functioning: the mental skills we need to plan, organize, regulate attention, manage impulses, make thoughtful decisions, stay motivated, and reach our goals. It's teaching the hidden rules of the world. All those unspoken expectations that shape how we move through school, work, and relationships. For many students, especially those with lagging skills, these things don't come naturally. So instead of punishing them for not knowing, we teach them. We front-load. We model. We give them the *how*. Because the social world is complex. And it only gets more layered as we get older.

SEL is not about compliance. It's about competence. It's not about making kids behave but helping them belong. We don't just praise the students who come to us with these skills naturally developed; we meet every child where they are and build their social-emotional capacity. When we teach SEL well, we don't just create better classrooms—we create better humans.

But getting to that point meant I had to shed some old versions of myself. No more people-pleasing, playing it safe, or going along to get along. I had to step into something new, something that required me to be brave even when I didn't feel fearless. I had to head toward the challenges instead of away from them. And that's what led me to the role I have today.

Here's what I know for certain: You're facing your own storms too. Different circumstances, same crossroads. The question isn't *if* challenges will come—they always do. The question is *who you'll become* when they arrive. Will you run from them, or will you turn and face them head-on? Because there's a version of you on the other side of that decision. One that's been forged by the very thing you're tempted to avoid. That's why I'm here to help you become the BISON. To help you stop running from the storm and start running through it.

— CHAPTER 3 —

Becoming the BISON

Yep, you read that correctly. A bison. You know, the animal? You see, I had an incredible coach once tell me about the thing with bison. When there's a storm, cows will run away from it. They see the lightning, they hear the thunder, and they're afraid, so they head for shelter. But bison herd together and run *into* the storm. They see that lightning, they hear that thunder, and they know that the fastest way to get out of it is straight through it. They're brave. They're bold. They're freaking fearless. And that's because they know how to act with intention. That intentional action gets the attention of fellow bison. And guess what? That group becomes a herd. That's what being the BISON is all about: *being intentional so others notice.*

Listen, we can tell our team members to be more collaborative, but that doesn't mean they're actually working together. We can ask our partners to be more supportive, but we can't make them choose genuine care. We can demand accountability from colleagues all day long, but we can't force authentic ownership. And this is the exact challenge we face as educators every single day. We get so caught up in wanting to see the right behaviors that we completely miss the internal shifts that actually create lasting change. The BISON mentality? It's designed to bridge that gap. Because real educational leadership isn't about controlling what people do; it's about inspiring who they can become. That happens when we stop focusing on compliance and start focusing on connection.

THE BISON FORMULA THAT CHANGES EVERYTHING

Here's where *perspective-taking* becomes your superpower. The BISON mentality isn't just "be intentional"—anyone can tell you to do that. It's about being intentional in a way that creates genuine connection with the humans you're trying to reach.

Let me show you what this looks like in real life. A friend of mine went to pick up her son from camp, and at the closing ceremony, the camp leader went through every single child and shared some words about each. My friend couldn't wait to tell me all about it. She was absolutely glowing because this leader had told everyone that her son was "authentic and true to himself."

But here's what made this so powerful. This leader could have just noticed these qualities about each child and kept things to himself. Instead, he intentionally chose to share what he saw with the families because he knew how it would make them feel—seen, valued, proud. My friend wasn't the only parent who approached him afterward to thank him for really seeing their child and then sharing that gift with them. That's the difference between just noticing versus being intentional so others notice too.

Stop and think about someone important in your life. What do you want them to notice about you? Maybe that you care, that you're reliable, that you see their potential. Now think about how it feels when someone actually notices those things about you—that warm feeling in your chest, that sense of being truly seen. That's what we're creating for others.

When you actively listen during a tough conversation, you're helping someone notice that their voice matters. You're helping them feel genuinely heard. When you celebrate someone's effort publicly, you're helping them notice their worth and feel valued. This is perspective-taking in real life: stepping into someone else's world and designing your actions to create the emotional experience that actually drives change.

WE CAN'T ASSUME THEY JUST KNOW HOW

I recently met with the teachers in my SELebrate Good Times Community. We have veterans, novices, and everyone in between. We've been diving into Mel Robbins's book *The Let Them Theory*. Even as accomplished adults—people who teach students, lead teams, manage relationships, and make important decisions daily—we were having massive aha moments about how incredibly difficult perspective-taking actually is. And if *we're* still figuring it out, how can we expect others to naturally know how to do it?

This is exactly why the BISON mentality is so much bigger than goal setting or performance reviews. We're teaching perspective-taking through lived experience. When we consistently show up with the complete formula, we're not just hitting our goals; we're developing the emotional intelligence of everyone around us. They start to understand what intentional leadership looks like and how it feels to be on the receiving end of it. And that's when the magic happens. The people around you begin considering the emotional impact of their own actions, naturally becoming the kind of educators, leaders, mothers, fathers, spouses, and friends who understand that with great intention comes great responsibility.

What does it mean to be intentional in the classroom? It means front-loading conversations about emotions and behaviors rather than being reactive. It means making sure our classroom strategies are equitable and consistent. It means knowing that being flexible isn't a betrayal of your authority but an authentic response to what comes up in the classroom.

And you need to be intentional with yourself too. Instead of focusing on all the competing things on your plate, you've got to turn inward and start asking yourself this: Who do you need to *become?* Who do you need to become to live each day in your classroom like the badass you are? Who do you need to become to walk into your school with a sense of calm and confidence? Who do you need to become to start living each day as the teacher, administrator, or school leader you thought you would be? That you *want* to be right now?

And who do you need in your herd to make it happen? Because you simply cannot do this work alone. You need your champions. You need your ambassadors. You need people with clarity who value connection. And you need these types of leaders at every single school site.

When you start showing up intentionally for yourself, your students, your family, and the people you interact with throughout your day, your herd will naturally grow. Because this is when you start to build those true, long-lasting, loving, supportive, and dare I say *intentional* relationships. You can live in the ease and the flow of your profession. You can feel safe, valued, and understood, and you understand how to support *yourself* along the way.

This book is about stepping into a new way of teaching, one that doesn't rely on reactive discipline but instead front-loads expectations, embeds social-emotional learning into daily routines, and builds a foundation where students have agency, teachers feel empowered, and everyone is supported. We're shifting away from managing behavior to teaching the skills students—and adults—actually need. We're creating a classroom culture where students don't just follow rules; they understand *why* they matter. And they understand this because these rules have been taught, modeled, and reinforced with intention.

It all starts with us. With deciding, before the chaos, how we want to feel. Then we take intentional steps to create that reality. This is the BISON mentality. Because bison don't wait for conditions to change. They move forward, knowing they have the strength to withstand whatever comes their way. They don't run from a storm. They run into it, together. Becoming the BISON is all about reminding yourself how you want to feel before you allow the heaviness to start settling in. Then you take control, take action, and run with your people, your herd.

What I've learned as a teacher, educational leader, coach, mentor, mother, and wife is that there's something more important than being fearless when the storm rises: choosing courage in the face of fear. You must recognize when the skies start to shift, know the steps that ground you, and be sure you have the strength to take them. Most of all, you must realize that we were never meant to face it alone. Humans, like bison, were programmed to move together.

Take a deep breath. We're all going through something. Life is tough to talk about sometimes. Maybe your position is on the chopping block due to budget cuts, or perhaps beloved programs at your school are disappearing without warning. Maybe you and your administrator aren't seeing eye to eye, or your team feels more like a collection of silos than a true support system. Perhaps a new curriculum is being rolled out with little direction, or the big behaviors in your classroom are starting to wear you down. I know it's overwhelming, but you are not alone. There is light ahead, and the change you so desperately seek is not only possible—it's truly within reach.

This, right here, right now, is the moment you choose to become the BISON. It's the moment you stop running away and start taking intentional action toward the change you want to see, one intentional step at a time.

Throughout this book, we're going to explore how being intentional and being noticed work hand in hand. Because when you act with purpose, really thinking through how your actions will land with others, you create moments when people feel genuinely seen and valued. And when others notice the positive impact you're making, it fuels your confidence to keep taking those brave steps forward. It's a cycle that builds on itself: Intentional action leads to meaningful connection, which gives you the courage to be even more intentional in the future.

BISON is more than just an acronym. It's the formula for a complete shift in being, in becoming. And I'm going to walk you through exactly how to make this transformation happen. To *be intentional so others notice.*

We'll start by stepping into change, acknowledging where you are right now and getting clear on where you want to go. Then we'll talk about prioritizing yourself; you can't pour from an empty cup. From there, we'll dive into taking action and the specific, intentional moves that create real change in your classroom, your school, and your relationships. We'll explore how to find your herd, the people who will support and amplify your efforts. And we'll discuss how this ripples out to families and your broader community. Because when *you* change, everything around you has the potential to shift too.

Here's what I want you to remember as you're reading: You are at the center of all of this. The change starts with you, but it doesn't end with you. Every intentional step you take creates a ripple effect that touches the lives of your students, your colleagues, and everyone in your orbit. You have more power than you realize, and this book is going to help you step into that power with confidence and purpose. So let's begin by doing what bison do best. We're running into the storm, together.

PART II

Running INTO THE STORM

— CHAPTER 4 —

The Magic of INTENTION

The magic happens when intention becomes the foundation of everything you do. This isn't about being perfect or having all the answers; it's about being deliberate in your choices, thoughtful in your actions, and purposeful in your interactions.

When you're intentional with your tone of voice, your responses to challenging behavior, your conversations with families, and even the small moments that fill your day, something shifts. People begin to notice a difference when they're around you. They feel more connected, more valued, more inspired. It's not forced or performative. It's genuine, and that authenticity is what draws people in.

But here's what I need you to understand: You're not being intentional so others will notice and praise you. You're being intentional because when you act with purpose and care, the people around you feel the difference. They can't help but notice because they're experiencing something real. Think about how you want them to feel, then act with intention and purpose that aligns with that feeling. When you do this, people start to experience genuine connection, authentic care, and an intentional investment in their well-being.

When intention becomes integrated in your daily systems—your teaching strategies, your conversations with students and families, and even the phrases you use throughout the day—that's when the transformation begins. Not just for others but for you too. Because living with intention doesn't just change how others experience you. It changes how you experience your own life and work.

Your colleagues walk down your hall and feel the magic spilling out of your classroom. Your administrator can't help but sit down and start interacting with your students. And it's not because they're visiting to check up on you; it's because they want to be part of it all. They want to feel the magic, the love, the energy that you're pouring into the lives of the students who are lucky enough to be with you each day.

The families of your students will start to thank you. Not for teaching their children how to solve math problems or write persuasive essays. Not for covering the curriculum standards or preparing their kids to take that dreaded state test. While those things matter, that's not what moves parents to reach out with genuine gratitude.

Instead, they're thanking you because their child came home excited about learning for the first time in months. They're thanking you because their shy kid finally feels confident enough to raise their hand in class. You took the time to really see their child—not just as a student but as a whole person. And you helped that child see their *own* potential. Parents are thanking you because you created a classroom where their child feels safe to make mistakes, ask questions, and be authentically themselves. I mean, I might bet that you've never been thanked for any of that, but I'm not a betting kind of person!

This is how we start to bridge gaps. It's how we create a common language with our families and encourage a long-lasting, genuine, sustainable, and incredibly connected community across the country. It's the BISON mentality, and it starts with you. From the inside out. We're bringing the herd together to head straight into those storms, but like the bison, we begin with ourselves, in our own space.

Your classroom is where this transformation takes root. The walls that surround you, the scents that fill the air, the colors you've selected, and the countless choices you make each day. Do they support you in the way you had hoped? If not, what are you going to do about it? What can you change? Because you need that support every single day. You need to feel the calm. You need to feel at ease. And here's the truth that changes everything: You are in control of these things.

You are in control. You get to choose. But first you must create the foundation. You need a calm, centered space that will sustain you through every storm that comes your way.

FIND THE CALM

By this point you're probably asking yourself just what the heck I mean by acting intentionally. Let me start by asking you a simple question: How do you react when things don't go as you had originally planned? Don't even think about a classroom setting just yet. Take this slow.

Let me share a story that perfectly illustrates what it means to find your calm in the middle of an unexpected storm. I'm starting with something that has nothing to do with education because this is where the real practice happens. Not just in the classroom. Not just during the school day. But in all the interactions that happen all around us in our world, with all the people we encounter.

The neighbor who leaves their lights on glaring through your windows all night. The family member who pushes your buttons at dinner. The friend who cancels plans at the last minute. The spouse who leaves dishes in the sink. These everyday moments, these ordinary interactions—this is where we build the emotional muscle we'll need when we step into our classrooms.

If you're reactive and emotionally dysregulated, you can't just flip a switch and suddenly be calm, intentional, and responsive in the classroom. The practice starts in the real-world moments that matter. This is what finding your calm looks like.

For a few years, my husband and I were part of what I thought was a fun neighborhood fantasy football league. Nothing too serious, just couples from around the area getting together for a lighthearted fall activity. I knew absolutely nothing about football, but somehow I won the league one year. Me? The dancer turned edupreneur? I had totally dominated a group of die-hard football lovers. Pretty badass, right?

All jokes aside, we were, like most people, incredibly busy. But we had carved out time to set our lineups, watch the games, text in the group chat, and cheer others on because we wanted to be part of something. We wanted that sense of community and connection.

Then, at the beginning of what should have been a new season, out of nowhere, I received a message asking us to remove ourselves and relinquish our spot in the league. Not only that, but this person, someone I considered a friend, told me they had been "thinking about our friendship." This brought in a whole host of other things that had nothing to do with fantasy football. The message was blunt, unexpected, and honestly, it hurt me.

All these emotions and thoughts came rushing through me. Had we stopped going over to their house to watch the games together? Kinda. I'd started traveling more, and my husband had gotten a new job that required him to travel too. On the days where we were back together at home, I just wanted to turn off my brain and love on my family.

My first instinct, though? I was pissed. I was sad. All these emotions came flooding in at once, and I could feel that familiar surge: wanting to react big, to fire back, to defend myself, to let this person know exactly how unfair and hurtful they were being.

But instead, I sat in how I felt. I let myself feel the hurt without immediately trying to fix it or fight it. I asked myself the crucial questions: What can I control here? What can't I control? What was the intention behind the text? What was their perspective on the situation? And what actions can I take to move forward?

I couldn't control this person's decision or the words they chose to use. I couldn't control their perspective or their feelings about our friendship. I definitely couldn't control their intention behind the action they took. But I could control my response. I could choose to keep my calm.

And that's exactly what I did. Instead of reacting from a place of hurt and anger, I took time to center myself. I found my calm, and from that place, I was able to respond with grace—not because this person deserved it but because I deserved to maintain my peace.

This is what finding your calm looks like. It's not about being passive or letting people walk all over you. It's about choosing your response from a place of strength rather than reaction. It's about protecting your energy and your peace, even when others (adults *and* kids) are determined, intentionally or not, to disturb it.

Because our reactions don't just affect us; they also affect the thoughts, feelings, and reactions from the people around us. This is what makes up our social world. And this is the adult version of social-emotional learning.

What you're practicing, what you're learning to do, is to act with intention. You're going to take an active role in regulating your emotions in order to respond in expected ways. And when we respond in expected ways, the people around us feel calm and comfortable, which makes them want to continue to be around us. This is how we create lasting friendships and relationships with people.

Now, will I likely be best friends with the people from that fantasy football league? Probably not. But here's the thing: We live in the same neighborhood. We'll see each other at community events, at the grocery store, at our kids' activities. How I chose to respond in that moment determined whether those future interactions would be comfortable or awkward, whether there would be tension or peace when our paths crossed.

This kind of social thinking is layered and complicated. And if it's this challenging for us as adults, imagine what it's like for our students. They're learning to do all this social thinking while still developing their emotional regulation skills. We must practice acting and responding with intention so we can teach our students to do the same. When we model this calm, intentional response, we're showing them that it's possible to feel hurt, process those emotions, and still choose how to move forward with grace. And don't worry, I'll get into the action steps you need to bring the calm into your classroom and home later.

RECOVERING PEOPLE PLEASER

There was a recent time when I didn't act or respond with intention. I was working with a well-known coaching organization, and two of my mentor teachers had gone out to support teachers at a school site. The feedback was incredible. Teachers were following us on Instagram, sliding into our DMs, and sharing stories about the transformations they were seeing in their classrooms and in themselves. I was so proud of the work we were doing.

Then the organization's director asked if we could talk. She wanted to give me feedback on what she had observed. One example she shared particularly stung. A teacher had tried something new, and at recess, she came running back to the staff lounge, bursting with excitement to tell my mentor teachers about her success. They celebrated her. They said, "This is incredible! Keep going! You've got this!" They were her cheerleaders in that vulnerable moment of trying something new.

But the director saw this as a "missed opportunity for teaching and growth." She criticized what I saw as beautiful, supportive coaching, especially on day one.

I was a recovering people pleaser who desperately wanted this director's approval. I wanted her to love our work, to give us more schools and districts across that county. And when I felt that slipping away, when she questioned my daily coaching of these mentor teachers instead of celebrating our results, I reacted. I got defensive. I argued from a place of anger and hurt instead of stepping back to find my calm and respond with intention. I let my emotions drive my response, and it showed me exactly what I didn't want to be: reactive instead of intentional.

You see, for so many years, practically my entire life, I thought I needed to become who people wanted me to be. I was a people pleaser, a perfectionist, a yes-girl riddled with anxiety. I would dim my light, shove it deep into a box, and perform just enough so that no one's feathers would ever get ruffled. I would shrink myself so that the people around me felt comfortable. I would do absolutely anything to avoid that uncomfortable feeling of not being liked, being ridiculed, mocked, talked down to, or even worse . . . threatened.

I was constantly turning down my volume. Don't be too loud because if you are, a colleague might snap at you in the lunch room for adding to their migraine. Don't take on too many leadership opportunities because it might come across as brownnosing. Don't hang up the student activities each month in the hallway because other people will feel like they're not doing enough. Don't be too perky as you walk through the halls because people will start to wonder if you're actually teaching.

I continue to be a recovering people pleaser, like so many educators are. We want to do the right thing. We want to feel like we're good enough, that we're making a difference. When I moved from the dance world to teaching full time in the classroom, I grabbed any opportunity I could get. I took a position as an intervention teacher when schools weren't hiring full-time teachers. And because there's never enough space in schools, I would find anywhere I possibly could to work with my students. We posted up in the hallways, corners of the library, at any available table and chairs, or even on the floor. I made it work wherever we could find a spot because that's what people pleasers do.

So what ended up happening? Some of my colleagues went directly to the principal and complained that I was being too loud and disrupting their students. Here's the irony: Through the glass windows of *their* classrooms, I could see their students sitting like robots while the teacher stood at the front of the room, separated by distance and desks, talking *at* them. Silent. Still. But my animated teaching? The laughter between my students and me? And the volume of my voice? That was the problem. As a people pleaser desperate to fit in and be accepted at this school, I was devastated. I questioned everything about myself and my teaching.

Fast-forward a few years. I had moved to a different school and a different district. My son and I were at our local frozen yogurt place. He was busy creating his perfect combo with way too many toppings, and I was waiting by the counter. The young woman at the register spoke up: "Are you Mrs. Gameroz? I think I had you as my teacher in sixth grade." She was beaming, and I got full-on body chills. This girl I had worked with for just two hours a week in a small math intervention group remembered *me*? But truly, you know what she remembered? She remembered my voice. That loud, animated, fun-loving voice that had gotten me in trouble. And you know what else? She also remembered how I made her *feel*.

Although constantly feeling like I needed to conform to others' expectations was exhausting, looking back, I realize that my years of people-pleasing were an essential learning experience. They taught me that trying to please everyone—your administrator, parents, colleagues, district—is not only impossible but soul-crushing. As educators, we're constantly pulled in different directions, trying to meet everyone's expectations while losing sight of what we know is best for our students and ourselves.

Now, when I work with educators across the country, I see this same pattern everywhere. Teachers burning out because they're trying to be everything to everyone. They're second-guessing their instincts, dimming their light, silencing their authentic teaching voice because someone might disapprove. But here's what I've learned: Embracing exactly who you were meant to be as an educator—loud voice, laughter, animation, and all—is not just your superpower. It's what your students need most.

The key isn't conforming to everyone else's expectations. The key is learning to be flexible while staying true to your core.

FLEXIBILITY IS KEY

"They just don't know how to *do* school."

I'll never forget one of my clients telling me this at the beginning of her school year. And I get it. Some of our kids have lagging skills, and others are lacking them entirely. You might have a student who has a difficult time sitting on the carpet listening to their teacher teach. Why? Probably because they're used to looking at an iPad or a Nintendo Switch or a TV that's constantly throwing rainbows and Roblox in their faces. If they lose interest in something, they change it. And when they search for something new, they have a world of options at their fingertips.

Back in the day, we didn't have that. If we wanted to search for something, we had to drive to the library and *search* for it. And then if we wanted to make sure we had that information, we had to copy it on a copy machine. I mean, think about that. Really think about it. If we wanted to watch TV, we were only able to watch what was on our basic cable channels. And that's *if* we had cable! Some of us even had to actually get up and turn the dial if we wanted to watch another channel, maybe even fiddle around with the antenna so the screen wasn't all fuzzy.

Isn't it absolutely insane to look back at what life used to be like? There was no TikTok, Instagram, or AI. No one knew what reels were, or social media. Uber and Netflix didn't even exist. And now that's all taken on a life of its own. Our children were born into a world where this is just how it is. You want to watch something, google it. You want to listen to something, tell Alexa. Want to go shopping? Add it to your cart on Amazon. Need to respond to that dreaded parent email? Plug it into ChatGPT. It's just so wild how much we have at our fingertips and how quickly we're able to attain new information whenever we want.

And that's having a significant effect on the brains of our students. They were born into a world with immediate gratification, constant input, and access to anything they can possibly think of *all the time.*

They're able to go from one thing to the next almost instantaneously. And to put it in more technical terms, they don't have to *work* their working memory. And by *work*, I mean *werk*.

You see, your working memory is your brain's Post-it note. You know how you write down all the things you need to remember to do? And then you cross them off or rearrange them in the order that makes the most sense? Then when everything on the Post-it is crossed off, you take out another one and do it all over again.

Your working memory, that Post-it note in your brain, hangs on to all your plans, all those steps you need to take, all the things you need to do in order to reach your goals all day long. And those goals can be as minute as getting dressed or driving to Starbucks, or they can be as lofty as planning an extravagant vacation or writing a book. And believe me, writing a book is a big goal.

But if I don't know how to work my working memory, then there's no follow-through. I'm not able to complete these tasks. I'm driving to work and getting so lost in thought that I miss my exit. I'm filling in an entire worksheet and leaving half the questions unanswered. I'm taking a test but my mind is going completely blank. I'm writing this damn book but can't keep track of all the moving pieces and chapters that need to come together.

The problem isn't that we don't know what needs to be done; it's that we don't know the steps we need to take in order to do it. Which means we can't put them in the order they need to be in. A student might know they need to make a craft project, but they glue the pieces together before cutting them to the right size. Maybe they start writing an essay without first organizing their thoughts, leaving them with a jumbled mess instead of a coherent piece. As adults, we do the same thing. We might start cooking dinner before checking if we have all the ingredients, or maybe we begin a presentation without outlining our key points first.

When our working memory skills, or *executive functions*, are lagging, we lose our motivation halfway through tasks. We get tired from the mental juggling act of trying to hold multiple steps in our mind simultaneously. We become dysregulated when things don't go as planned, and we get off track because we can't maintain our focus on the end goal while managing all the details. We might need to shift our plan midstream, but without strong working memory skills, we can't adapt, so we just abandon ship entirely, leaving behind a trail of unfinished projects and unfulfilled commitments.

And it's not only our working memory that has changed. Remember how we used to have little toy trains that we'd push around the room while making *choo choo* sounds? We were using our imagination and our motor skills, and guess what was happening while we played? The little wires in our brains were connecting. Neural pathways were forming, and our brains were wiring in a way that made other things less tricky for us.

Then came new trains that moved by remote control and emitted electronic whistles. With this evolution of the toy train, we took away our kids' ability to use their imagination and make the sound, but we also took away their ability to push, move, and glide this train around. And what does this do? If we take away imagination *and* we inhibit a child's ability to exert their gross and fine motor skills, what happens to their brain?

Yep! It gets wired differently. Here's the scary part. Are you ready? Think for a second. Where are the toy trains now?

You guessed it! They're on the iPad. They're on the cell phone. They're on the TV. In fact, not only are our children just sitting there watching toy trains, but they're watching other kids play with toy trains!

We've completely removed the imagination, the movement, *and* the interaction with others.

So my question to you is this: What are we going to do about the fact that our current students' working memories are depleted and their brains are wired totally differently than ours were a few decades ago? Can we simply banish the world of technology and assume that students must learn the same way we did? Nope. The reality is that technology is just going to continue to morph. It's up to us to be flexible as these changes continue.

If you're closed-minded or rigid, or if you're comfortable and set in your ways, then SEL cannot take place. It just won't. Because when your emotional intelligence is stuck, your students' emotional growth will stay stuck as well. And no learning at all will take place.

So we need to intentionally practice flexibility ourselves. Try taking a different route to work tomorrow, even if your usual way is faster. Order something new from your regular coffee shop instead of your go-to drink. When a lesson plan falls apart midclass, resist the urge to power through. Instead, I want you to pause, breathe, and tell your students that things aren't going as planned. Maybe even ask them what they think should happen next. This can feel calm, and everyone can move forward. Practice saying, "I don't know, but let's figure it out together" instead of feeling like you need to have all the answers. These small acts of flexibility in low-stakes situations build our capacity to stay open and adaptive when it really matters—and it *really matters.*

To address kids' rigid thinking patterns, try activities that deliberately disrupt their expectations. Play games where the rules change midway through. Give them art projects with mystery materials they've never used before. Present them with problems that have multiple right answers, then celebrate every creative solution they discover. When they insist "that's not how we do it," respond with curiosity: "What if we tried it this way today? What might happen?" These moments teach them that uncertainty isn't dangerous; it's where growth lives.

Trust me, I'm a girl who thrives on predictability and consistency, but the reality is that the only constant in this world is change. And when those changes come, the strong might survive, but the flexible, the *intentional,* will thrive. We know we want our students to be flexible thinkers, have a growth mindset, and persevere. But we must model these things for them first. That is how we create the change we want to see in the next generation of educators, families, and children. It's up to us.

LET'S TALK ABOUT BEHAVIORS

Now you may be thinking to yourself, "That's all great, Kim, but how can I get to the point of doing SEL work when my students are jumping on tables, biting their peers, or hiding underneath their desks?" It's a great question, and believe me, I've been there.

What about students who wander around the classroom staring at the lint in the air? How about the ones who walk ever so slowly, taking the long way to their desk so they can watch the hand sanitizer drip through their fingers down onto the carpet? Anyone? Anyone? Or maybe you're dealing with students who constantly call out, interrupt lessons, or make silly noises to get attention. Perhaps you have kids who shut down completely, put their heads down, and refuse to engage with anything. Maybe there's a student who seems to push your buttons deliberately, or one who has a meltdown every time you ask them to start their work, declaring, "I can't do this!" before they've even tried.

Here's another scenario that might sound familiar. Let's say you have a student named Marcus who has an intense special interest in dolphins. Like, he's *obsessed* with dolphins. Your class is doing a research project where students work in small groups, and each group picks an animal to study. Marcus desperately wants to research dolphins, but another group already claimed that topic.

Now you're faced with a choice: Do you force him to stay in the group that's working on penguins to be "fair" to everyone else? Do you avoid teaching him how to negotiate and collaborate with his peers because it's easier to sidestep the chaos that could ensue? Or do you let the disaster movie play out—watch him melt down, scream, maybe run out of the room—and then call the front office when he starts tearing posters off the walls?

What's fair in a situation like this, and what's equitable? And what's fair to you when you don't have the skills to deal with what might unfold? This is where understanding the difference between fairness and equity becomes crucial to teaching with intention and consistency.

Fairness means treating everyone exactly the same. Everyone gets the same worksheet, sits in the same type of chair, follows the same rules in the same way. It sounds good in theory, but it doesn't account for the reality that our students come to us with vastly different needs, experiences, and challenges: social, emotional, physical, neurological, etc.

Equity, on the other hand, means giving each student what they need to be successful. It recognizes that equal treatment isn't always just treatment. In an equitable classroom, some students might get flexible seating while others sit at traditional desks. Some might need movement breaks while others need quiet spaces. Some might need extra time while others need enrichment activities. We do these things because it's literally what their brains and bodies *need.*

There's a brilliant lesson that many teachers use at the beginning of the school year, and it perfectly illustrates this concept. The teacher asks students to raise their hands if they've ever scraped their elbow, and everyone does. She picks one student to tell the story of how they scraped their elbow, then puts a Band-Aid on their elbow. Next, she asks if anyone has ever bumped their head. When hands go up, she has someone share their story, then says, "I am so sorry you hurt your head. Here's a Band-Aid for your elbow." Then she asks about scraped knees and again responds, "I am so sorry you scraped your knee. Here's a Band-Aid for your elbow."

By this point, the kids are completely confused. The teacher stops and has a conversation about how even though she gave everyone the exact same thing in the exact same way, it wasn't helpful to most of them. A Band-Aid on your elbow doesn't help a bumped head, a scraped knee, or even a broken heart. As she explains to her students, "Fair doesn't mean everyone gets the same thing. Fair means that everyone gets what they need so they can keep going and be successful." It was fair that everyone got a Band-Aid, but it wasn't equitable because it didn't solve their actual problems or meet their real needs.

Going back to our Marcus example, equity might mean allowing him to research dolphins, if that's what helps him engage and participate in the learning process. It's not about lowering expectations; it's about removing barriers so he can meet those expectations. Fairness would force him into the penguin group because "you get what you get, and you don't throw a fit." Equity recognizes that his success in learning collaboration skills and research techniques matters more than which marine animal he studies. This is UDL. This is SEL. This is just good teaching.

When we teach with equity as our foundation, we're being intentional about meeting each student where they are. We're being consistent in our commitment to every child's success, even when that consistency looks different from student to student.

Many of our teachers feel lost when facing these challenges. It's exhausting just running through scenarios in your head, and oh boy, when the chaos actually happens in real life, yes, that's truly exhausting.

But here's what I want you to know: Believe it or not, despite having students who started the year acting out in all the ways described above, my classroom ended up in a completely different place year after year. My students were happy. We were a community, and all my kids thrived.

And it's not just my story. I work with teachers every day who are going through these same challenges. The table jumping, the work refusal, the meltdowns, all of it. But when they approach these behaviors with the right systems and the right mindset, they experience the same transformation I did. Their classrooms shift from chaos to calm, from struggle to success.

How do we get there? How do these teachers create this change? This transformation doesn't happen overnight. It's a gradual process that requires patience, consistency, and a fundamental shift in how we understand behavior.

I had a special education teacher say it perfectly when our teaching community met over Zoom. She said, "It's always going to be one of two things. When you see big behaviors in your classroom, ask yourself this: What are they trying to communicate, or what do they need to help themselves regulate?" I thought it was so beautifully put. It's that simple. It comes down to communication and regulation.

Think about it. When a student is calling out constantly, they might be communicating "I need attention" or "I don't understand and I'm afraid to look stupid." When a student is wandering around the room, they might need to regulate by moving their body because sitting still feels overwhelming. When a student refuses to work, they might be communicating "This feels too hard and I'm scared to fail," or they might need regulation strategies to manage their anxious thoughts.

And here's the reminder that changes everything: It all begins with a focus on you. We have to focus on ourselves as the adult in the room first and use the tools in our toolbox so we can respond from a regulated space. Then we can check in with our students and see if it's a need to communicate or a need to regulate.

My whole point is that if you want a calm classroom, it has to come from you first. You're the only one who can change your classroom culture. Your students are looking to you to set the tone, to be the steady presence they can count on, to model the regulation and communication skills you want them to develop.

In fact, as I type this, I'm staring down at the keyboard of my computer, and I have a single Post-it stuck right by the mouse. Do you want to know what that single Post-it has written on it? "No one is going to change your classroom except for you."

That's not meant to add pressure. It's meant to empower you. You have more influence over your classroom environment than you might realize. And when you approach behavior from a place of curiosity instead of frustration, when you see it as communication instead of defiance, when you respond from regulation instead of reaction, everything begins to shift.

The beautiful thing is that once you start this work, your students will follow your lead. They'll begin to feel safer, more understood, and more capable of success. And that's when the real magic happens. But it's going to take more than just understanding behavior as communication. Your students need to know exactly what you expect from them, and they need explicit instruction on how to meet those expectations. As much as we'd love them to simply absorb our SEL and classroom culture through osmosis, the truth is that our students are not mind readers. And that's exactly what we'll explore next.

OUR STUDENTS ARE NOT MIND READERS

Some of our most frustrating moments as teachers come when students don't act the way we want and expect them to in a given classroom situation. You know, like when a student walks into your classroom after recess, still buzzing with energy, and instead of transitioning smoothly to the next part of your school day, they're talking loudly to their neighbor about the epic kickball game, rummaging through their backpack like they're searching for buried treasure, and seemingly oblivious to the fact that twenty other students are already quietly settled at the carpet with their whiteboards and dry erase markers ready for the math lesson.

Sound familiar?

Here's what you need to do. Instead of continuing to hope that your students will simply read your mind and conform to your unspoken expectations, you need to let that wishful thinking go. Don't create expectations for your students, any of your students, without first explicitly teaching them what is expected of them in every social situation at school.

Teach social and emotional skills. Don't expect them.

Write that down.

Because here's the truth: The majority of our students are still trying to figure it out. They're navigating complex social dynamics, learning to manage their emotions, and developing the executive functioning skills they need to succeed. And they're doing all of this while trying to master academic content. So instead of expecting that they'll magically figure it out on their own, we need to teach them.

We must model, role-play, and front-load conversations about all possible scenarios before they happen. We must give students solutions and strategies before problems even arise. We must help them set realistic goals and celebrate their growth, no matter how small that growth may seem. This work happens all day long, in every interaction, in every transition, in every moment of connection.

I know it sounds daunting, but trust me, the intentional work you put into explicitly teaching these skills to all your students will come back to you tenfold. It's how you build a community of empathetic, lifelong learners. It's how your students develop true grit and a growth mindset. It's the power of being intentional with your teaching and embracing a proactive rather than reactive mentality.

And here's the beautiful part: When you do this work consistently, other people will notice. Your principal will notice the calm energy in your classroom. Other teachers will ask what your secret is. Parents will comment on how much their child loves school. Most importantly, your students will thrive in ways that extend far beyond your classroom walls.

IT'S NOT JUST ABOUT THE STUDENTS

Being intentional is not only about doing what's best for your students. Sure, that's a great and important outcome. But to get there, you need to do what's best for you first.

Let's start with something as simple as the space you occupy. Think about your classroom, your office, or even your home workspace. Is it a place you actually want to be? Think about the colors that are in there, the things you have posted on the walls. Does it feel like home? Does it feel like a place where you're going to do your best creating? Does it feel like a place where you will build incredible relationships with little humans? Does it feel good to you? Does it make you smile when you walk into that room every single day?

The question I have for you is simple: How do you want to feel, and what do you need to do to your space to feel that way?

When I'm in my office at home, I want to feel a sense of calm and peace. But I also want to feel energized and rejuvenated. It's a mixed bag over here, what can I say? And it probably is for most of you too. I want to feel the ocean breeze mixed with the scent of rosemary, and I want the view of Hawaii while living in Texas. I can truly only get one of those things. I'll make it easy for you: There's no ocean around me, and it's either hot and humid or cold as hell most of the time.

But I do my damnedest to create an environment where my needs are being met. You better believe that when I go to my favorite restaurant and walk into that bathroom and smell that rosemary candle burning, I walk out with one or two to add to our bill. I've got pictures of palm trees and everything else I could find from our last trip to Maui, plus room spray that literally smells of ocean and plumeria all bottled into a perfect little concoction of island paradise.

When you create a space that nurtures your soul and meets your emotional needs, you show up differently. You're calmer, more creative, more patient, and more present. And guess what? Your students will feel that energy the moment they walk through your door. They'll sense that this is a space where good things happen, where they're welcomed, and where learning and love take place.

Don't underestimate the power of intentionally designing your environment. Whether it's adding plants for life and freshness, displaying student work that makes you proud, using lighting that feels warm instead of harsh, or incorporating scents and colors that bring you joy, these seemingly small choices create the foundation for everything else you want to accomplish. They're intentional and create a lasting impact.

When your physical space has order, your mental space follows. Everything in its place means your brain isn't working overtime trying to remember where you put things or what you forgot to do. It's freed up for the work that actually matters. You're not constantly searching, scanning, or feeling that low-level static of chaos. You can actually think. Because when you take care of your space, you're taking care of yourself. And when you take care of yourself, you're better equipped to take care of everyone else who walks into that space. It's not selfish; it's strategic. It's not superficial; it's foundational.

Your space should reflect the energy you want to cultivate and the relationships you want to build. Make it intentional, make it yours, and watch how it transforms not just your daily experience but the experience of everyone who enters your world.

But your space is just the beginning. What matters most is who you're becoming within it. This extends to how you think, how you lead, and how you navigate everything that comes your way. Do you want people to notice possibilities instead of limitations? What about unity instead of silos? Do you want to be the one who creates transformation instead of just hoping for it? Then you need to step into change. Over the next few chapters, I'm going to show you exactly how. Not just things to do but ways to *be* that will pull you forward into the person and educator you're meant to become.

— CHAPTER 5 —

Step into CHANGE

We've all been there. The days when it feels like we're not making a difference. Like nothing's changing. Like every day is a struggle. I've had days where I didn't think I was moving forward. Where the kids didn't seem to learn, the behaviors were too big, and the paperwork was never-ending. Progress often shows up in the smallest moments. And if we're not looking for it, we miss it.

But here's what I've learned: change is hard. Starting a new system, believing in it, staying consistent with it—those are some of the hardest things we can do as educators. They require us to step away from what's familiar and trust that something different might actually work.

One of the systems I implemented in my classroom was a check-in process where students would identify how they were feeling the moment they walked into the classroom. They'd tap an emotion on a chart, give it a label—angry, anxious, excited, tired—and then attach meaning to it. *Why* do I feel this way? What's happening in my body? Then they'd choose strategies they could use right then to support themselves. This happened every single time they entered the room, whether it was the start of the day or after recess.

In my eyes as a teacher, it was a consistent way to keep tabs on them—to get a glimpse into what was going on inside their brains and bodies. But it was also building something bigger: their self-awareness and self-management. Day after day, they were practicing the skills of noticing, naming, and responding to their emotions.

I'll never forget this one student I worked with. Every morning, without fail, he would come into school angry, clinging to his mom like a koala, refusing to let go. We'd literally have to pry him off her so she could leave, and even then, it felt like we were pulling him into the classroom, where he'd immediately start his day in fight-or-flight mode. I did everything I could to help him. I bought him all the Pokémon stickers and books he loved, trying to create a connection. I made sure to set up a special safe space for him in the room, a place where he could retreat when things got overwhelming. But still, day after day, it felt like we were stuck in the same loop. His outbursts disrupted the entire class, and I was running out of options.

One morning, something incredible happened as I watched him walk into the classroom. I could see the moment he caught himself beginning to lose control. Instead of immediately falling into his usual pattern, he paused. He checked in with himself about how he was feeling, then reached for the coping strategies we had been practicing together. There were days when these strategies worked and times they didn't, but this day felt different. What happened next was nothing short of miraculous. He walked into the classroom, took a deep breath, and actually stayed there. It was a small moment, barely noticeable to anyone else, but to me it was everything. I could see the wheels turning in his mind as he worked through his thoughts and emotions. And that was when I realized this student wasn't just trying to survive the day; he was learning how to manage it. It was a game changer, both for him and for me.

And here's the truth: If I had limited this student to what I already knew—the behavior charts, the sticker rewards, the working-toward-a-prize systems—I never would have seen this moment. Those things have their place, but *this*? This was the real reward. Watching a child step into change because of a system I believed in enough to stay consistent with.

If I had stuck to the old playbook, I would have robbed him of the chance to develop true independence. I would have limited his ability to regulate his emotions—a crucial skill every single one of us needs to navigate life. Instead, by stepping into change myself, I created space for him to do the same.

BE INTENTIONAL BY *stepping into change* SO OTHERS NOTICE POSSIBILITIES, NOT LIMITATIONS.

That's what was happening here. This is the BISON mentality. In this moment, I was stepping into change by allowing this new system to unfold. I could see that it was possible for this student to come to school and feel calm. Simultaneously, he was stepping into his own change and discovering that a school day could feel different. And his mom had to step into change too. She usually felt that she needed to control the situation instead of allowing her son to take the lead. We weren't limiting him or lowering expectations. We were expanding what we all believed was possible, and we all noticed.

As educators, we need to train ourselves to notice those small wins. Because the truth is that we're all doing the work—sometimes it just doesn't look how we think it should. Maybe your student isn't reading at grade level yet, but they chose a book during free time and actually sat there flipping through the pages and staying put. Maybe your child didn't master their multiplication facts, but they tried three different strategies on their own to solve the problem during their math test. Maybe that student didn't have a perfect day, but they walked away from conflict at recess instead of escalating and creating chaos. Those moments matter. They build resilience. And if we don't pause to acknowledge them, we miss the proof that we are moving forward.

Change is uncomfortable because it takes us into the unknown. And let's face it, most of us hate that. We like a plan, a road map, consistency, something we can count on. But true growth? Real transformation? That's what happens in the messy middle, the space where we don't have all the answers and we have to figure it out as we go.

I've had to step into change multiple times in my own career, and each time it was terrifying. When I transitioned from being a classroom teacher to working as a district coach, I had no road map. I was stepping into the unknown, working with educators I'd never met, in schools I'd never been to, trying to support growth in ways I'd never done before. It was uncomfortable, messy, and honestly, there were days I questioned if I was making the right choice. But if I hadn't stepped into that change, I would have limited not only myself but also all the educators I was meant to serve.

Then I did it again when I started my own business. I didn't know what I was doing. I had no business plan, no clear path, and definitely no guarantee of success. Of course it was scary and messy. But I had to step into change because I had allowed myself to notice what was possible, not just for me but for all the educators and school districts I could reach and support. Each time I chose growth over comfort, I didn't just transform my own possibilities—I opened doors for others to do the same.

Maybe you're in the middle of change right now. Whether it's in your classroom, with your own kids at home, with a spouse or friend, or maybe within your leadership team, my advice to you is to lean into the unknown. Try something new. Give yourself permission to not have it all figured out. Because none of us do. But the ones who are willing to embrace the unknown, the ones who are curious enough to take that first step? Those are the ones who make the biggest impact.

BECOME THE BISON

BE THE CALM IN THE STORM

Remember how I paused before reacting to that fantasy football text message? That split second of intentional calm? That same principle applies to every moment of chaos in your day. When the storm is swirling around you, chaos everywhere, the most powerful thing you can do is hold steady. And I know it's not easy. When everything's falling apart, it's so tempting to react, to lose it. Trust me, I lose it all the time. But when you do that, when I do that, the whole room follows your lead. Your students, your team, your family—they're all watching. They're all noticing. They're picking up on your energy. Because feelings are contagious. You can't help it.

Let's be real. The challenges will keep coming. The workload won't magically disappear. The students will still struggle. The obstacles will remain. But how we experience those challenges? That part is up to us.

People love to tell us to "just take care of ourselves," as if a bubble bath or a five-minute meditation is going to magically fix the exhaustion, the overwhelm, or the relentless pace of what we do. To be honest, when someone asks me about my self-care routine, I have to fight the urge to roll my eyes. Because what does that even mean? Another thing to add to my to-do list? Another expectation I'm supposed to meet in the middle of an already impossible situation? No thanks. Instead of obsessing over self-care, let's focus on something that actually works: creating clarity and space to think and making intentional choices in the moment.

Marc Brackett talks about taking a *Meta-Moment*—pausing in the middle of the chaos to ask yourself, "How do I want to handle this? What is the best version of me in this situation?" Dan Siegel often refers to the concept of the *hub* and returning to this space rather than getting sidetracked by surface-level behaviors. Mel Robbins uses the *let them theory* to help us remember what we can and can't control and to take action. We're talking about the *BISON mindset* here in this book. And we're all trying to say the same thing in different ways.

When a student is screaming, when a meeting goes off the rails, when your child is pushing every button you have, what will you look back on and be proud of? That pause, that moment when you step outside the emotional tornado, is everything. It's not about pretending the chaos isn't there; it's about deciding that you won't add to it. The storm can rage, but you don't have to get pulled into it. That's what being the calm really means. Not stuffing down your frustration, not forcing yourself to smile through gritted teeth, but choosing, intentionally, to stay steady, neutral, at ease. Not adding more fuel to the fire.

For educators, this might mean slowing your breath before responding to a student who's testing every ounce of your patience. For parents, it might be reminding yourself that your child's meltdown isn't personal. It's *their* struggle, not a reflection of your failure. For leaders, it's about keeping a clear head when emotions run high, modeling the kind of presence that makes others feel safe and capable. And when you make that choice to hold steady, others feel it. They take cues from you. Your students, your kids, your team—they see that you're not reacting. You're responding. And that gives them permission to do the same.

So no, I don't want to talk about self-care in the way people usually do. I don't want to be told to "light a candle and take a break," although I do love candles. What I care about is learning how to stay grounded when it matters most. Learning how to show up in the way I want to be remembered. Learning to remember what I can control so I can take intentional action. That's what makes the difference. That's what being the calm in the storm really looks like.

FLIP THE SCRIPT

Change blindsides us. One moment, we're confidently following our carefully crafted lesson plans, our school routines, or even our parenting strategies, and then suddenly, something shifts. A new curriculum, an unexpected leadership change, a diagnosis, or a world-altering pandemic forces us to rewrite the playbook. And in those moments, we have a choice. We can resist and sink deeper into frustration, or we can flip the script and find a way forward.

This isn't about toxic positivity or pretending challenges don't exist. It's about choosing to see possibilities where limitations once stood. For educators, this might mean seeing a challenging student not as a behavior problem but as a child desperately in need of connection. For parents, it might mean recognizing that your child struggling in school isn't a sign of failure; it's an invitation to advocate, adapt, and uncover new strengths.

Flipping the script starts with a pause. When change hits, our instinct is often to react. We want to push back, to complain, to resist, to defend, to make excuses. Instead, take a breath and ask a question: "What is this change trying to teach me?"

During the pandemic, my role as a district coach was flipped upside down. I was working alongside teachers in their classrooms, and suddenly, it was over. No one was at school. There were no kids to support in classrooms. No teachers to work with in person. I had to abandon my expectations of "normal" and instead ask, "What can I control?" I could control how I chose to show up for the teachers and families across the district. I could control how I supported colleagues drowning in the same storm. And I could control how I modeled resilience: Instead of pretending I had it all figured out, I could be real about the struggle and show how I chose to move forward anyway. Educators who flip the script in their classrooms teach kids an invaluable lesson. Life won't always be predictable, but our responses to change define who we become.

If you're a parent watching your child struggle socially or academically, flipping the script means shifting from "Why is this happening to my child?" to "What strengths is this challenge revealing?" If you're a leader facing resistance to a new initiative, it means moving from "Why won't they just get on board?" to "How can I communicate the vision in a way that inspires?" The key to flipping the script is intention. When you intentionally shift from a mindset of frustration to one of curiosity, you create space for growth, not just for yourself but for those watching you. And when you step into change with intention, others notice. Suddenly, what once felt like chaos becomes an opportunity to innovate, pivot, and grow.

SELEBRATE THE SMALL WINS

Social-emotional learning happens in moments. They're the quiet, often unnoticed moments that can easily slip by if we're not intentionally looking for them. When we SELebrate, we're not just offering generic encouragement or celebrating compliance. We're recognizing and honoring the emotional growth and self-awareness that takes place within each person.

That morning when I watched my student walk into the classroom, pause, check in with himself, and choose to use his coping strategies? *That* was SEL in action. His self-awareness kicked in when he recognized he was starting to lose control. His emotional regulation emerged as he accessed the tools we'd practiced. His cognitive flexibility led him to stay in the classroom instead of fleeing. This wasn't about following rules or meeting academic expectations. This was about emotional growth, and it deserved to be celebrated, or SELebrated, as such.

SEL celebration looks different from traditional praise. Instead of "Thank you for sitting in your seat," it sounds like "I noticed that you're listening with your hearts and calm bodies right now. That makes *me* feel so calm and respected." Instead of "Great job, you got all your work done," it becomes "I love how you advocated for yourself when you raised your hand because you knew you needed support. How does *that* feel?"

For parents, SELebrating might mean acknowledging when your child expresses their feelings instead of bottling them up, even if those feelings are difficult to hear. It's recognizing when they show empathy toward a sibling, when they bounce back from disappointment, or when they take responsibility for their actions. These are the building blocks of emotional intelligence.

As leaders, we can SELebrate when team members show vulnerability in admitting they don't know something, when they navigate conflict with grace, or when they demonstrate resilience during challenging times. We're honoring their social-emotional learning journey, not just their productivity.

The truth is that for many of our students, and even adults, mastering these social-emotional skills can take a lifetime. Self-regulation, empathy, emotional awareness, healthy relationships—these are complex, ongoing areas of growth. And when we pause to SELebrate the small steps in this journey, we're not just offering encouragement. We're validating that this internal work matters, that growth is happening, and that each small win is building toward something bigger.

This is how we create momentum. This is how the BISON keep running. This is how we help people see their own progress and continue moving forward in their social-emotional learning journey.

FIND THE SILVER LINING

Life is never on cruise control. It doesn't just glide along smoothly, letting us sit back and relax. It throws curveballs. Big ones. And when it feels like challenge after challenge keeps coming, it's easy to slip into frustration, exhaustion, and even resentment. "Why does this keep happening to me? Why do I always have to be the strong one?" Believe me, I've asked myself those same questions. But here's what I've learned: Every experience, especially the hardest ones, shapes me into a stronger, wiser, more capable version of myself. And while I don't always *want* to be the one who has to push through, I know that every challenge I've faced has given me something I wouldn't have had otherwise: a deeper understanding, a sharper skill set, and a story that can help someone else down the road. Trust me, I've got stories for days.

As educators, we don't just get the kids we *want*. We get the kids we need. You might want to read that again. The ones who test our patience, challenge our thinking, and force us to grow? Those are the students we need. And not just for one year. Not just so we can kind of step into the challenges and experience growth. These are the experiences that we need over and over and over again. You need the tricky ones. You need the tough ones. You need them, just like they need you.

I was recently with a teacher who looked around her classroom and saw students with trauma, students with extreme behaviors, students whose social and emotional struggles made learning feel impossible. She said, "Why do I keep getting *these* kids?" But the truth is that she wasn't being burdened with these students. She was being trusted with them. These children were meant for her, and she was meant for them. Just because their behavior might have been challenging the year before didn't mean it would stay that way. And because she leaned into the work instead of resisting it, she built strategies that made a difference. Now she can mentor colleagues, support families, and advocate for kids in a way that only someone with her experience can.

Finding the silver lining doesn't mean pretending everything is fine or ignoring the struggle. It means asking, "What is this teaching me? How is this shaping me?" Maybe it's forcing you to develop more patience, to build stronger systems, or to become the kind of leader who can speak from real experience. Maybe it's giving you a perspective that will help someone else down the road. Maybe it's preparing you for something bigger than you can see right now. If certain kids didn't have us, who would they have? They're meant to be with us for a reason. And I am a true believer of that.

We don't always want to be the strong one, but if we've been given these challenges, it means we're capable of rising to them. And that is powerful. When everything feels overwhelming, pause and ask yourself this: "What am I being given here? What will I be able to do because of this experience?" You might not see it right away, but the silver lining is always there, waiting to transform both you and the students you're meant to serve.

EMBRACE THE UNKNOWN

Change is uncomfortable. It forces us into places we've never been, asking us to let go of certainty and step into something we don't fully understand. And if we're being honest, that's terrifying. As educators, parents, and leaders, we often crave structure. We want to know the plan, the outcome, the guarantee that things will work out. But real growth? Real innovation? It happens in the space where certainty doesn't exist. When we choose to embrace the unknown instead of resisting it, we give ourselves permission to discover new possibilities we never would have seen otherwise.

For parents, this might mean trusting that your child's struggles are not setbacks but stepping-stones to something greater, or perhaps just different. It might mean leaning into a new parenting approach, advocating differently, or letting go of the need to control every outcome. For leaders, it might mean taking risks that challenge the status quo, knowing that real change only happens when we are willing to disrupt what no longer serves us. The unknown is uncomfortable, but it is also where the magic happens.

When you choose to embrace the unknown with courage, others notice. Your students see it. Your colleagues feel it. Your children learn from it. They watch you navigate uncertainty, and in doing so, they gain the confidence to do the same. Because the reality is none of us have all the answers, but those who are willing to step forward anyway are the ones who change the game for everyone.

I can remember thinking, "I was just a teacher in a classroom." I had never mentored educators before, worked at a district office, lived or moved out of state, started a business, given a keynote, started a podcast, created a website, or written a book—until I did. And here I am, doing all these things. I'm coaching and working alongside educators all across the nation, giving them opportunities to do this work they've never done before either. I paved the way for them.

My family is watching, the educators in my coaching community are watching. The unknown is scary. Who knows what will happen? I have a vision, an action plan, and high hopes, but there is no certainty of the outcome. And that's exactly the point. By stepping into the unknown anyway, it changes the game for everyone watching. They see that it's possible to begin something new, to take risks, to move forward without guarantees, and to create opportunities for others along the way. That gives them permission to do the same. And you can do it too.

— CHAPTER 6 —

Prioritize YOURSELF

Before I started coaching educators across the country, I was completely terrified of traveling—specifically, flying. It scared the crap out of me. The thought of stepping onto an airplane, let alone doing it regularly, felt impossible. But I had this vision, this pull toward something bigger: helping teachers across the nation feel seen, supported, and equipped to handle the challenges in education. I remember talking to my neighbors about it one evening, sharing my dream but also admitting how paralyzing the idea of flying was. The husband, who happened to be a pilot for American Airlines (which, by the way, is the airline I fly all the time now), looked at me and said something I'll never forget: "You know you gotta get on an airplane to do this, right?"

He was right. If I wanted to do this work, if I wanted to reach educators and make an impact, I had to get on the plane, over and over again. As much as I wanted to avoid it, I knew deep down that it was necessary. And that's exactly what I think about when I hear the phrase *put your oxygen mask on first.* Just like flying, taking care of yourself might not always feel easy or natural, but it is absolutely necessary.

Think about an airplane emergency. The instructions are always the same: If the oxygen masks drop, you have to put yours on first before helping others. Why? Because if you pass out from lack of oxygen, you're useless to the people who need you. That same principle applies to teaching, parenting, and leading. Your classroom doesn't run without you. Your students don't learn without you. You are the heartbeat of that space. But if you're running on empty, if you're exhausted, drained, and overwhelmed, you can't give your best to the people who depend on you. And let's be honest: When you're at your breaking point, everyone around you feels it.

When I talk to a new group of teachers, I open with something simple. Tell your students how *you* want to feel in your classroom. Ask them how *they* want to feel. And then come up with a list of steps you *all* will have to take in order to feel that way. It's easy to focus on what students need, but your needs matter too. If you want a calm, focused environment, you have to be calm and focused. If you want joy, you have to cultivate it. That means protecting your energy, setting boundaries, and recognizing that you set the tone. Your well-being is not an afterthought; it's the foundation of everything else.

So, what does it look like to put your oxygen mask on first? It means recognizing when you're running low before you hit burnout. It means setting boundaries with your time and energy instead of pouring from an empty cup. It means being honest with yourself about what you need to feel fulfilled, not just functional. And most importantly, it means leading in a way that shows others—your students, your children, your colleagues—that prioritizing yourself is not a luxury but a responsibility.

When you operate from a place of intention, rather than depletion, everyone notices. The light you shine is different. You breathe life into the rooms you walk into, and people feed off that energy.

An educator friend of mine recently described me on his podcast as "a ball of energy," and he said that I breathe life into the people I connect with. That's who I am. I can't be anything other than that. It's special. Those are two of my superpowers. But I can't continue to pour that energy into other humans if I don't protect my energy first. Neither can you. That's the kind of educator the world needs more of, and that's exactly who you can choose to be.

PUT YOUR OXYGEN MASK ON FIRST

Too often, as if there's some sort of checklist, the world asks, "What are you doing to take care of yourself?" For educators navigating chaos in their classrooms, that question can feel like another thing we're failing at. So let's reframe it: What can you do to reclaim even a sliver of your energy? Maybe it's pausing to breathe before you respond to a student. Maybe it's recognizing the small moments of joy, like a smile or even a smirk, from a kid who usually avoids eye contact, the silence of your classroom after dismissal, or the taste of your coffee on a hectic morning, even if it's turned cold. That is intentional living. That's the real self-care.

Because the chaos isn't going away. The big behaviors, the shifting expectations, the endless to-do lists, the parents questioning your every move, the administrators piling on new initiatives—they're all still there. They'll always be there. But you get to choose how you show up.

You know that story about the snakebite? When someone gets bitten by a snake, they don't waste time chasing after it, demanding to know why it bit them or trying to convince it that it was wrong. They focus on treating the bite. They focus on survival. They focus on themselves. Yet somehow, when life bites us, when that difficult student pushes every button, when your administration tosses another curveball, when parents send an email that makes your stomach drop—we do the opposite. We chase the snake. We exhaust ourselves trying to control things that were never ours to control in the first place. Meanwhile, the real work—taking care of ourselves, protecting our energy, staying true to our purpose—gets ignored.

Taking care of yourself isn't selfish. It's survival. It's also the difference between showing up with fulfillment or showing up with nothing left to give. And no, I'm not talking about bubble baths and yoga classes, unless those genuinely fuel you. I'm definitely a yoga fan. I'm talking about making intentional choices that make you the main character of your story again. Because when you lose yourself, you lose your purpose. You lose the spark that drew you to this work in the first place, and you're no longer bringing that main character energy to this world you live in. And I'm a big fan of people who bring that main character energy.

There's something about teaching that draws us in. There's this promise of shaping little minds, helping them grow, and being the positive influence they need. But let's be real. Sometimes that promise gets hard to hold on to. We'll always have students who test our patience, whose behaviors seem to come from another galaxy, whose needs feel overwhelming. And let's not even get started on the outliers. There are also the kids who don't fit into our neat little boxes or follow the playbook we so carefully crafted. We dig deep into our bag of tricks, trying everything we can think of to help, but it only works for a minute before we're right back where we started.

And when our bag is empty? The frustration builds. Then we hit a wall. No more strategies, no more tools, no more phrases. We're exhausted, overwhelmed. And in the midst of it, we still get more on our plates. There are changes to the curriculum and constant shifts in the grading system. The pendulum swings again, and there's a new focus, a new initiative, just when we'd gotten comfortable with the last change. It's exhausting. And it feels endless. But I've learned an important lesson.

BE INTENTIONAL BY *prioritizing yourself* SO OTHERS NOTICE FULFILLMENT, NOT BURNOUT.

That's the secret. And when you live like this, everything falls into place.

Think about it. Emotions are contagious. When you walk into a room carrying the weight of burnout, everyone feels it. Your students sense your exhaustion before you even speak. Your colleagues absorb your stress during team meetings. Your own family feels the heaviness you bring home. But when you show up fulfilled, when you've put that oxygen mask on first, people are drawn to your energy. They want to be around you. They want what you have. Your students respond differently because they're not trying to navigate around your frustration. Your colleagues seek you out because you bring solutions, not just complaints. You become the person others turn to, not because you have all the answers but because you've figured out how to stay whole while doing this work. That's the kind of educator, the kind of person, who changes everything. Now let me show you how to do it.

BECOME THE BISON

SET BOUNDARIES, NOT WALLS

I can't stand the phrase *work-life balance*. It's everywhere. It's always plastered on motivational posters, thrown around in professional development sessions, used as a catch-all solution for burnout. But let's be honest: Balance feels like pressure. It suggests that if we just shift things around perfectly, we'll somehow achieve this magical equilibrium where everything in our personal and professional lives is evenly distributed, neatly stacked, and perfectly managed. That's not real life. Life isn't balanced. It's messy, unpredictable, and constantly shifting. What we should be striving for instead is harmony. Just saying the word *harmony* makes you feel lighter, doesn't it? It's about creating a rhythm that works for you, where the pieces of your life complement each other rather than compete for your time and energy.

And part of creating harmony is knowing when to say yes and when to say not right now. That's where setting boundaries, not walls, comes in. I don't love the word *boundaries*, either, but I do love the idea of making intentional choices that protect your energy without shutting people out. When we put up walls, we're closing ourselves off. It's like slamming the door to our classroom, shutting our office door, or pulling down the blinds at home. We're creating distance. The truth is that we need connection. We need people. Teaching, parenting, leading—these are deeply relational roles. But that doesn't mean we have to be available to everyone all the time. It just means we have to be intentional about what we say yes to so we're not left exhausted, resentful, and stretched too thin.

I always tell teachers, "Do what feels good for you." Does grading written assignments at home make you feel more at ease? Or does it make you feel like work is bleeding into every corner of your life? Is that stack of papers a tab open in your brain, running in the background and keeping you from being fully present? If closing that tab means you can show up as a fun mom, best friend, partner, sister, or just a human being without the weight of unfinished work pressing down on you, then close it. But if leaving it open helps you feel more in control and less stressed the next morning, then by all means, keep it open. The point isn't to follow someone else's idea of balance. It's to create a sense of harmony that works for you.

So take the time to think about what drains your energy. What are the things that keep you from feeling fully present in the moments that matter? What are the expectations, from yourself and others, that feel more like walls than open doors? Setting boundaries isn't about rigid rules. It's about protecting your capacity to show up for the people, and the work, that matter the most to you. It's about making intentional choices that allow you to live and lead with clarity, energy, and ease. That's harmony. And that's what will sustain you in this work, in relationships, and in life.

NURTURE YOUR AUTHENTIC SELF

The first time I was introduced to a personality assessment, I was in college, sitting in a class where we were learning about the Myers-Briggs Type Indicator. I remember being fascinated by how a simple test could offer so much insight into the way I think, work, and interact with others. Later, when I was a teacher working as a district coach, the Enneagram became the big thing. Everyone was talking about it—what number they were, what their wing was, how it explained their strengths and struggles. And now, as a business owner, Human Design has entered the conversation. I'm a Manifesting Generator, which honestly makes so much sense given the way my brain works and how I constantly dream up multiple ideas *and* take action to bring them to life. Even my husband, in the business world, has taken the DiSC assessment to better understand his leadership style. The point is that there are so many tools out there to help us uncover more about ourselves. And if you've never taken one of these assessments, stop reading for a second and go take one. There are tons of free options online, and you'll only need a few minutes. You might be surprised by what you learn.

But learning about yourself isn't just a fun exercise; it's a way to harness your superpowers. And taking action with this knowledge is the only way to nurture them. Too often, we take personality tests and think, "Oh, that makes sense," and then we move on. But what if we used this information? What if, instead of seeing our natural tendencies as things that just make sense or things we need to change, we leaned into them? All of them. These assessments aren't meant to put us into a box. They're meant to help us understand why we act the way we act so we can operate from a place of self-awareness and strength. What I've learned as I've grown is that self-discovery is about more than just knowing your type. It's about aligning who you are with what you value and then stepping into action that reflects your authentic self. Now *that* was a mouthful.

As a teacher, understanding yourself allows you to reflect on why you do things a certain way in the classroom. Maybe you thrive on structure and consistency, or maybe your strength is building relationships and making learning feel like a conversation. If you know that your superpower is creating an engaging environment, you can lean into that while setting a goal to also strengthen your classroom management if that's an area that's lacking. Because when you know your strengths, and your weaknesses, you can be intentional about using them and also recognize where you might need to grow.

As a leader, whether in a school, district, or business, know that your leadership style helps you better connect with those around you. Are you a visionary leader, always coming up with big ideas? Are you the one who thrives on systems and processes? Or maybe your superpower is supporting and encouraging others to reach their full potential. The more you understand your natural strengths, the more you can use them to lead with confidence while also recognizing when to lean on others who have strengths you don't.

And as a parent, this self-awareness is just as powerful. Maybe your instinct is to plan everything out and keep things structured, or maybe you go with the flow. Perhaps your strength is in listening and making your child feel safe, or maybe it's in teaching independence. When you know your own tendencies, you can embrace the way you parent while also being mindful of how to adjust when needed.

The beautiful thing about embracing your authentic self is that it doesn't just transform how you show up; it transforms how you connect with others. When you understand your natural strengths and areas for growth, you can recognize the same in the people around you. Instead of being frustrated by differences, you start to see them as complementary pieces of a bigger puzzle.

This is where real support happens. Maybe your colleague thrives on big-picture thinking while you excel at details. Perhaps your partner is naturally encouraging while you're great at problem-solving. When you know yourself well, you can step in to support others from your strengths without losing yourself or getting frustrated, angry, or overwhelmed in the process. But this is crucial: You can only give from a full cup. Supporting others should energize the team, not deplete you.

That's why taking the time to truly know yourself matters so much. Find out what energizes you, what drains you, what feels right in your soul, and then make intentional choices to honor those things. Because when you embrace your true self unapologetically and fully, you don't just give yourself permission to be who you really are—you give others permission to do the same. We create spaces of trust, honesty, and real connection. And connection is where all learning begins.

FILL YOUR CUP WITH GRATITUDE

When people talk about gratitude, you'll always hear them mention the gratitude journal. And honestly? It bothers me. I mean, I get what they're trying to do, but it just doesn't capture what gratitude really is for me. It's not about forcing yourself to write down a list when it doesn't feel natural to you. It's about living in a state of appreciation, especially when it comes to the connections we make with people.

I learned this lesson big time when my family moved from Southern California to Texas. Standing in line at Trader Joe's here feels like an hour-long event sometimes. But people ask you about your day and what you're cooking, and you get to know them on a deep level. I come back and ask the guy who passes out samples about his family and their dogs. I talk to the checker or the person bringing back the carts about what happened over the weekend. I'm not just talking about the weather—because these are real people with real stories. And I'm grateful for them.

It's the same at the farmers market downtown. I know the stories of the farmers who grew the produce, and these people take the time to really get to know you. If you don't have enough cash to purchase both of those cartons of eggs on a Saturday morning, every single one of those merchants will tell you, "No big deal. I've got you. You can pay us back next week." It just feels different here. Less like a rat race, less like being stuck on a hamster wheel. Slower. More connected.

What fills *my* cup is appreciating the people I encounter, whether it's a colleague in the hallway, a student in a classroom, or someone I meet at the grocery store. But here's what I've figured out: Appreciating people isn't about complimenting them. It's about being present with them. It's about listening with your heart, not just with your ears. Sometimes when you're sitting with somebody, you don't even need to know what to say next. Just sitting with them is what they need. And as an educator, coach, mentor, or parent, this is really difficult for a lot of us to do.

To appreciate the people around us, we can't depreciate ourselves. We need to give ourselves credit for the work we're doing, the relationships we're building, and the growth we're experiencing. And if you're reading this book, you are experiencing growth.

I watched this reel on Instagram where Oprah Winfrey was talking about filling your cup with gratitude so much that it begins to overflow, and then it runs over and spills out to the people who matter to you the most. That's exactly it. As your cup overflows, it spills into the lives around you, and it transforms your perspective. People start to see your growth and your energy, and you begin to inspire others to do the same thing.

So instead of waiting for the perfect moment to reflect or jot down gratitude items, instead of forcing yourself to do something that doesn't feel natural to you, just appreciate the unexpected conversations that happen throughout the day. Appreciate the students who bring joy, and challenge, into your life. Gratitude isn't just an inward practice; it's an outward practice too. It's about connecting, listening, and truly valuing the people you interact with. This is what fills your cup, and more importantly, it's what allows your energy, your love, your passion, and your values to overflow into the world around you.

SELEBRATE YOUR JOURNEY

Listen, teachers message me all the time and say, "Kim, I had the worst day ever." And I get it. Our kids do the same thing. They walk through the door and immediately launch into saying, "Oh my God, it was literally the worst day of my life." But here's what I want you to do (and this is going to take some practice). I need you to stop and really ask yourself some questions: Was it actually a terrible day? Like, the entire eight-hour school day? The whole twenty-four hours? Was every single minute awful? Or was it one terrible conversation, one frustrating moment, one bad experience driving from point A to point B? Sometimes we let one crappy moment define our entire day, and that's just not the reality of what happened.

And here's another thing: Celebrating your journey isn't about sitting around waiting for someone else to pat you on the back. You're not waiting for your principal to notice the email you sent to a parent or your spouse to say, "Wow, thanks for folding the laundry for us." Nope. This is about you recognizing your own wins. It's about creating this habit where you stop and say, "You know what? I showed up today. I took action." And those action steps don't have to be huge, life-changing moments. Sometimes it's as simple as thinking, "I'm so proud of myself because I took a deep breath before I responded to that text message." That's it. That's growth right there.

Let's go back to that fantasy football situation I was in. I could have completely lost it, but instead, I was proud of how I handled myself. I knew I needed to put my phone down and just feel everything I was feeling. Be disappointed. Be hurt. But then I remembered what I could control versus what I couldn't, and I was able to respond without all that emotion driving the conversation. Can I tell you something? One of the hardest things we can do is put distance between ourselves and whatever's triggering us. Every fiber of our being wants to react immediately. But that space? That's where the magic happens. That's where you grow. It's when you can pause, reflect, and then choose your next move instead of just reacting.

This happens in the classroom too. A student makes a comment that gets under your skin, or they move slower than molasses when you're already running behind schedule, or they don't complete their work again despite your reminders, or you walk back into a room that looks like a tornado hit it. In those moments, when every fiber of your being wants to snap, if you can take that deep breath and respond with calm instead of reacting with frustration, SELebrate that.

If you can have a conversation the next day with your students and come up with a solution together instead of just laying down the law, SELebrate that too. These aren't small victories. They're huge social and emotional wins, both for you and for your students, who are watching and learning from you how to handle stress, disappointment, and conflict. Every time you choose calm over chaos, you're modeling the exact skills you want them to develop.

This is exactly what I built my businesses around. I create communities across schools, across districts, and across the nation where educators celebrate their growth in teaching. They celebrate having less anxiety. They celebrate the small wins, the little changes within them, starting a new strategy, having an intentional conversation that used to take twenty minutes out of their school day and now it only takes two minutes—and creates impact.

So here's what I want you to do. Start creating this sustainable practice of giving yourself credit where credit is due. Recognize when you're growing. Celebrate it. Tell yourself, "Yeah, I've got this." Because that energy you're putting out there? That's what we want our kids to feel too. We want them to have that confidence and self-awareness. They're watching us, and if we're not doing it for ourselves as adults, how can we expect them to do it for themselves as kids?

— CHAPTER 7 —

Take ACTION

This is probably my biggest thing right here. This is the hill that I will die on. Because there was a time when I would sit in meeting after meeting after meeting. I was part of committees after committees after committees, PD after PD after PD, and no action would follow. Back then, I couldn't really figure out what was bothering me every single time. But there was this feeling, this gut feeling within me, and I wanted to crawl out of my skin.

I know now it was because there was no action. I can't stand when teachers are asked to spend hours at the district office creating a mission statement or doing icebreakers to get to know a colleague. It feels pointless when nothing actionable comes from it. If we're going to invest that time, give me something I can actually use—something rooted in action that makes a difference in my classroom, my students' lives, or my school. Talking and thinking aren't enough. Show me what I can actually do.

BE INTENTIONAL BY *taking action* SO OTHERS NOTICE TRANSFORMATION, NOT COMPLACENCY.

Because when you take action, you enable transformation. Things start to change in classrooms, schools, districts, and homes when consistent action is taken. And other people notice this transformation. They notice that you weren't being complacent, that you weren't just sitting around talking about what could be different.

There comes a point, whether you're standing in front of a classroom, leading a district, or raising a child, when you realize that waiting for change is no longer an option. My favorite part of the film we created for Teaching Inside Out is when Jen, a third-grade teacher from the school district we were working with, says, "Nobody was going to give me the support I needed. I needed to reach out. I needed to take action." I could watch that part over and over on YouTube all day long. It literally gives me full-on body chills every single time.

And it's because she could feel the pull. Something inside of her knew that change was needed in her school and across her district. But transformation didn't begin with a massive overhaul. It began with intention. With deciding that who she wanted to be, and what she wanted to build, was worth the risk of discomfort. Being intentional by taking action means showing up not perfectly but purposefully. Because passivity has no place in a world that desperately needs your leadership, your heart, and your courage. And Jen—boy, did that woman have courage.

Too often in education and in life, we confuse motion with progress. We check boxes, attend meetings, implement new strategies, but deep down, we feel stuck. Complacency is sneaky. It masks itself in busy schedules and surface-level compliance. But transformation? It's loud. It's visible. It's felt. And not just by us; it's also felt by the students who enter our rooms, the staff who walk our halls, the families who trust us with their children, and the children watching us from across the kitchen table. When we choose to take intentional action, we send a message: Change lives here. Growth happens here. I'm not waiting. I'm moving.

Transformation is not about being the loudest voice in the room or launching a dozen new initiatives. It's about showing up consistently in small, brave ways, taking one honest step forward, even when your legs are shaking. It's about being willing to try, fall, reflect, and rise again, not just for the sake of productivity but for the sake of purpose. It's not just about what we're doing but about who we're becoming. The kind of transformation that changes a culture begins with the transformation we allow in ourselves.

This work takes courage. Real courage. Not the kind that gets applause but the kind that lets you walk back into the storm day after day with your eyes open and your heart engaged. Educators and leaders are often told to "just hang in there," but what we really need is permission to move forward. To disrupt what's not working. To speak up, step up, and create something better. That's where the shift happens, not because the system changed but because you did. And when that inner shift is real, it can't help but ripple outward.

That transformation we're after? The kind that changes classrooms, schools, homes, and hearts? It doesn't come from waiting for the perfect moment. It doesn't wait for the grant money to come in or the board of directors to approve the contract. It doesn't wait for the perfect group of students or for the tough year to pass. It comes from saying, "I'm ready now." It comes from moving with intention, even when it's messy. The power is in the action. Because when we take that first step—and then another, and another—people start to notice not just what we're doing but who we're becoming. That's when real change begins: not with policies or programs but with people who refuse to be complacent. People like you.

You need a lifeboat, not a kickboard. You need a community that helps you navigate the rough waters. You're not meant to be alone in this work. The beauty of this community, the herd of BISON, is that we're all in it together. We don't leave anyone behind. We celebrate our victories, no matter how big or small, and we lift each other up when it gets tough. Community is where the power lies. When you surround yourself with others who are also embracing growth, taking small steps forward, and stepping into the discomfort of transformation, you create an energy that pushes everyone forward. You grow together. You cheer each other on. And you create a momentum that's unstoppable.

So, you have to ask yourself this: Will you let the discomfort stop you? Or will you choose to embrace it as part of your growth journey? Will you take that one small step today, knowing it's part of something bigger? Because I promise you, this is how the change happens. One small step at a time.

And guess what? It gets to be easy. When you lean into the support and guidance of your community, when you focus on that progress, and when you make growth a daily choice, the storms become easier to face. Yes, you'll still have challenges, but you'll have the tools, strategies, and support to handle them. And when you feel supported, you have the energy, and the mindset, to keep moving forward.

BECOME THE BISON

START WITH ONE SMALL STEP

I'm living this right now. I'm in the middle of writing a book, recording for my podcast *Unleashing the BISON*, and launching the new *ViBE EDU Podcast*. I have my very first conference coming up in a month out in Southern California, and my teacher retreat in Wyoming, the Bloom, is in just two weeks. There are so many moving parts. I'm meeting with photographers and videographers, there are sets, displays, designs, presenters, sponsors, travel arrangements, social media, email lists. It's all pouring into our community. There's so much going on, and this is summer.

I was on a recent Zoom call with my photographer, Sarah, who comes to all our events, and she looked at me and said in the warmest voice, "One step at a time." It hit me: In those moments when you're staring at everything you need to accomplish, you can't just jump to the end product. You truly will only get there when you go one step at a time.

You know, starting with one small step is a powerful way to initiate change, especially when the journey ahead feels overwhelming. As educators, leaders, and parents, we face challenges every day that feel really hard. Whether it's improving student behavior, transforming a school culture, or just figuring out our own personal growth, true transformation doesn't happen overnight. It begins with one small, intentional action.

In your classroom, that one small step could look like trying a new teaching approach, even if it feels scary. It could be writing that email to your administrator asking for support. It could be forming that committee of teachers who are on the same page as you, where you know that real change could happen and you could shift the culture across your campus. It could be having that tough conversation with your kid that you've been putting off.

We look at our children and students, and sometimes we just want to change the behavior that makes us feel uncomfortable. We see them acting out and we want it fixed now. But what if we took their perspective? What if their small step is just learning to identify what they're feeling? What if their small step is asking for help instead of melting down? We can't expect them to jump to perfect behavior when we haven't given them the tools to take those smaller steps first.

These small actions build the foundation for something way bigger. What matters most is that we show up, take the first step, and embrace the uncomfortable feelings that come with growth. When we choose to take action, no matter how tiny, we send a message to ourselves and everyone around us.

We are role models. The small actions we take can inspire those around us. Our colleagues, students, or even our own children. The new teacher looking up to you for guidance, the aide who's learning from your classroom management strategies, or a student teacher who's learning about the profession by watching you. They are all looking to you. They're thinking, "If they can do it, I can do it." Your intentional actions set the stage for their growth as well.

It's not just about what you accomplish. It's about how you create change by embracing discomfort and taking that first step forward. When we focus on progress, however small, we build a community that grows together. And that creates momentum that is hard to stop.

So, no matter what, we need to start with one small step. Take it today and watch how it ignites transformation. Not only within yourself but also in those who are looking to you for inspiration. Because you most definitely are inspiring someone right now, even if you don't know who they are.

LEAN INTO DISCOMFORT

You know what? Many of us struggle with embracing discomfort as growth because, let's be honest, discomfort feels awful and we naturally want to avoid it. But I've learned that resistance, that fear, that nervousness you feel? It's usually a sign that you're stepping out of your comfort zone, and that's exactly where real growth happens.

Think about it. Every time you feel that sense of unease, it's probably because you're pushing yourself to do something new, to expand what you can do, or to try something that's going to stretch you. When we lean into that discomfort instead of running from it, we're opening ourselves up to learning and transforming. Those are the moments when we experience the most growth—because on the other side of that discomfort is the new version of ourselves. More skilled, more resilient, and ready to take on bigger challenges.

I'll be the first to admit that stepping into new situations makes me nervous every single time. Before I fly out to support schools in districts where I don't have any connections, I'm filled with doubt and fear. I'm nervous about walking into classrooms I've never seen before. I'm worried that my strategies won't work as well in this new place or that I won't connect with the principals and teachers who have never worked with me. I'm scared that this district won't be like the last one, that I won't be able to make the same impact.

But I remind myself that this discomfort is just part of the process. It's part of growing, learning, and getting better at what I do. In those moments of fear, I tell myself that I've learned from past experiences, and I can apply that knowledge in new ways. By embracing the discomfort, I open myself up to new opportunities for learning and growth that I couldn't have imagined from the safety of my comfort zone.

As educators, parents, or leaders, we all have those moments when we feel fear or resistance, especially when we're stepping into unknown territory. But if we want to model growth for the people we lead, whether it's a new teacher, a student, or a colleague, we have to show them that growth happens through discomfort. I've learned that when we lean into those fears and take action anyway, we're teaching the people around us that courage isn't about being fearless. It's about facing fear and doing it anyway.

It's okay to be scared, but it's also okay to take action. Over time, you'll find that as you face these uncomfortable moments head-on, you'll fear less. Your mindset will shift from seeing obstacles as roadblocks to viewing them as opportunities to develop new strengths. You'll start to approach challenges with excitement, knowing that each step you take gets you closer to becoming a better version of yourself.

And here's what I love about this: As you embrace this growth, you'll notice that you can more easily handle the tough stuff, both in and out of the classroom. You'll realize you're more confident, and you'll feel excited for what's possible.

LOOK AT THE GAIN

It's funny. Sometimes when we're reading a book about professional growth and development, we don't even realize that we're also working on our personal growth at the same time. This book isn't just about leveling up as an educator; it's about leveling up as a person. It's like when you think you're just buying a pair of shoes, but they come with a bonus. Maybe they make you walk taller, feel more confident, and put some pep in your step. That's what this journey is like. You're investing in yourself not only to be a better teacher or leader but to become a stronger, more resilient individual. So yes, you're reading a professional development book, but you're also signing up for a personal transformation. You're leveling up in both areas, whether you realize it or not.

But here's where we mess up. We're always looking at the gap. We're constantly thinking about what's next, what we haven't accomplished yet, what we still need to do. We're constantly focused on what's next, whether it's earning Teacher of the Year, achieving PBIS Platinum, or even making sure your child hits every milestone on time: walking, talking, winning that soccer game, getting into the right college, landing that perfect job. We're so focused on the future, on that next big thing, that we forget to look back at all the incredible things we've already accomplished.

What if instead of always staring at that gap between where we are and where we want to be, we took a moment to look at the gain? What if we celebrated how far we've come? Every small win counts, and it's so important to acknowledge these achievements. You might have had a tough week with your class, or maybe you've been working nonstop to hit a big target. Take a step back and say, "Look what I did." Think about how far you've come and honor that progress.

It's so easy to overlook our own progress when we're constantly focused on what's next. But sometimes we need to pause and recognize how much we've already accomplished. Take a moment to give yourself credit. This version of you. The version who can speak confidently in front of their colleagues, who has navigated tough challenges with their family or spouse, who has made it through a particularly challenging school year. That version of you is stronger than you realize. And that strength, that resilience, deserves to be celebrated.

It's not only okay to take a moment to look back and reflect on how far you've come; it's essential. *You* did this. And you need to SELebrate yourSELf, your own social-emotional learning, your own growth, your own progress. Because focusing on the gain instead of the gap? That's how you keep moving forward with confidence and joy. That's how you become the BISON.

CULTIVATE A COMMUNITY OF COURAGE

I don't know about you, but I want to surround myself with like-minded people. People who are curious, who are open, who have courage and are ready to step into action. I'm talking about the ones who will challenge you to think big and will hold you accountable when you're not staying true to your growth. Not the ones who will put you in your place and make you feel like you've made a mistake—the ones who will hold space for you.

I see this every day in the community over at SELebrate Good Times. These are teachers who are exhausted, who feel like they're drowning in their classrooms, who question if they can continue teaching. They're dealing with behaviors they've never seen before, admin who don't get it, and frustrated parents. They're going home every day wondering if they can do this for another year. But here's what's amazing: Out of their own teacher salary, they're still investing in themselves and a community. They're investing in their own personal and professional growth. And we all know what a teacher salary looks like across the country. But they are stepping into change because they know something has to shift. They are taking those small steps. When I ask them to consistently look at the progress they've made, they reflect and take action. And then I give them their next steps.

Maybe you're not ready to step into a community like that yet. That's okay. That first step could be as simple as listening to *Unleashing the BISON* or another podcast that resonates with you. I mean, seriously, even just following a podcast so that it pops up when a new episode drops—that's a step. Or you could join our Facebook group, Becoming the BISON, or perhaps another group that resonates with you and your values. It could be following people on social media accounts, whether it's LinkedIn, Instagram, TikTok, or whatever platform vibes with you.

But it could also be taking a bigger step—joining teacher or other retreats for in-person connection. And if you're not in education, it could be classes that you take, like Pilates or my yoga class that I absolutely love. I'm connected to the people in that class because we are like-minded. Just being around them fuels my soul. The room makes me feel good. The smells. Everything about it. Maybe it's a book club. Maybe it's a running group. Maybe it's a parenting group where you can share struggles and victories.

The key is finding your people, the ones who will support your growth and hold you accountable. Not in a harsh way, but in a way that says, "What happened? What did you do? And what are you going to do next time?" These are the people who celebrate your wins with you and help you learn from your setbacks. They're the ones who remind you of your goals when you forget and who cheer you on when you're taking those uncomfortable steps toward growth. No one necessarily needs to have all the answers, but the conversations you have and the things that you do are all small steps toward action and courage.

When you cultivate a community of courage, you're not just surrounding yourself with people who think like you do. You're surrounding yourself with people who challenge you to be better, who support you when things get tough, and who hold you accountable to continue to grow into the person you're becoming.

EMBRACE THE POWER OF YET

When faced with setbacks, challenges, or even the tiniest bit of self-doubt, it's easy to fall into the trap of thinking that things will never change. But here's a simple yet powerful shift that can make all the difference: Embrace the power of yet.

Instead of saying, "I can't get through to this kid," try saying, "I can't get through to this kid yet." Instead of "I don't know what to do to support them," try "I don't know what to do to support them yet."

By adding that one little word, you open the door to possibilities. It's a gentle reminder that growth is a journey, not a destination. When we embrace the power of yet, we don't just cultivate a growth mindset for ourselves—we change the mindset of the people around us.

In the classroom, one of the most important things we can teach our students is cognitive flexibility. Because flexible thinking doesn't always come easily, especially for some of our more rigid thinkers, but it's a lesson that sticks with them for life.

One of the first anchor charts I created for educators was about growth mindset and cognitive flexibility. My favorite was an anchor chart with three palm trees, all bending over in the wind. Picture a palm tree in Hawaii when a storm blows through—how those trees bend with the wind, never breaking. They sway, they lean, but they don't snap.

I'll never forget a video I got from a teacher who was asking the five-year-old student in front of her what it means to have a growth mindset. The little girl looked straight at the camera and said, "You know, be like a palm tree!" Then she curved her whole body over to the side with this "duh, of course" expression on her face. That's when you know it's clicking.

We teach our kids to be like those palm trees, flexible in the face of challenges, able to bend without breaking. But we've got to start practicing what we preach. It's not about avoiding difficulties but about learning how to navigate them with resilience. Whether it's juggling unexpected schedules or adding new responsibilities to an already full plate, flexibility doesn't mean giving up. It means learning to bend, to stretch, and to grow. Sometimes, it's about taking a deep breath and saying to yourself, "I haven't figured this out yet, but I will."

It's also important to remember that behaviors—ours and our students'—are often symptoms of something deeper. When you can't figure out why a child is acting a certain way, instead of getting frustrated, try shifting your perspective: "I haven't figured this out yet." Then take action. Drill down and understand why that behavior is happening.

When we model this for our students, we're showing them something powerful. That there's always room to grow, that there's always a way forward, even if we don't have all the answers today. Because we don't need to have all the answers.

Here's the thing about cultivating this mindset: When you embrace the power of yet, you're creating a community of courage around you. You're surrounding yourself with people who challenge you to be better, who support you when things get tough, and who hold you accountable to grow into the person you're becoming.

And speaking of your people, your herd, that's exactly what we're diving into next. Because growth doesn't happen in isolation, and the company you keep makes all the difference in the world.

PART III

Your HERD

— CHAPTER 8 —

Leading TOGETHER

I was just wrapping up a keynote. I had two of my mentor teachers with me, and one of the last slides I always show is a picture of me and my team, just the four of us, our small but mighty crew. All of us smiling, wearing splashes of pink. That picture always gets a reaction. Maybe it's the energy in our faces, maybe it's the intentional matchy-matchy outfits, maybe it's just how you can tell we actually like each other. Because we really do.

Those three are so incredibly special to me. We're so special to one another. It's just so rare to be able to look at someone and wholeheartedly, without a doubt, know that they've got this. I trust them. I know they exude good teaching. I've been in their classrooms before. I've watched them mentor and guide. I listen to them talk to teachers on the daily.

BE INTENTIONAL BY *leading together* SO OTHERS NOTICE UNITY, NOT DIVISION.

We're not trying to one-up each other. Nobody's trying to step on anybody's toes. Nobody's trying to advance their own career at someone else's expense. We are so united. We stand together. Whether all four of us are sitting there or not, we are intentional, and other people notice that.

This is what leading together looks like every day. Teachers know that they're going to hear from me, Debbie, Jenny, or Katie. They know that we're all going to say similar things and we're all going to back each other up. Even when we're standing there coaching groups of educators, we're going to finish each other's sentences. If one person is talking, the other person already has the anchor chart paper ready to go, and another one has already got the markers. We're so in sync with each other, and that's what leading together in a unified system looks like. People notice. They notice that this feels different. We're not divided. It doesn't feel fractured or competitive. It feels whole.

After one session, as people started gathering their things, a teacher made a beeline for us. She looked focused, like she had something important to say. She came right up to me and said, "Kim, I love everything about this. I love everything you're doing. But you have one problem." I braced myself. Oh no, here it comes.

She looked at me dead serious and said, "You don't have a blonde."

We all burst out laughing. She wasn't wrong. Every one of us in that picture is a brunette. It was a funny, lighthearted comment. But now, it feels kind of full circle. That teacher didn't just attend the keynote—she stayed connected. We ended up working in her district. She joined our coaching community. And recently, she shared something that hit me. She said she hadn't expected this to become such a safe space. A place where she could show up honestly, have real conversations about life and leadership, and feel deeply seen. Like she'd found her people.

That's what this is all about.

This work is bigger than strategies and systems. It's about connection. Collaboration. It's about realizing that we don't have to do any of this alone. Whether we're standing side by side or working miles apart, when we share the same mission, the same values, and the same language, you can feel the difference. I'll reiterate: Be intentional by leading together so others notice unity, not division. Because real transformation doesn't happen in isolation. It happens in community.

And sometimes? That community starts with a keynote, a pink outfit, and a joke about hair color.

BECOME THE BISON

SEEK DIVERSE PERSPECTIVES

Perspective-taking is more than just a reading comprehension skill that we teach our students. It's an essential leadership practice for building a culture of empathy, connection, and understanding. Everyone brings their unique life experiences to the table, and these experiences deeply inform how we engage with the world.

Early in my teaching career, I realized that supporting students with autism couldn't be done in isolation—not just in a speech pathologist's room for thirty minutes three times a week. Real progress required integration across all learning environments. But this understanding was just the beginning of a much larger lesson about the power of diverse perspectives in education.

Through my work connecting with educators across the country, I've discovered how profoundly different our contexts and experiences are. Teachers in South Dakota face completely different challenges than those in California, and educators in Washington navigate vastly different community dynamics than their colleagues in New Jersey. Some are first-year teachers finding their footing, while others have decades of wisdom to share. When you connect with educators from all these different places and backgrounds, you realize just how much there is to learn from one another.

The depth of these different experiences became even more real for me when I learned that one of the teachers in our community had experienced a school shooting in her district her first year of teaching. What she went through, and how it changed her, shaped not only how she approaches safety and emotional support in her classroom but also how she connects with students who carry their own struggles. Her perspective, shaped by something so difficult, offers insights that can't be found in any textbook or professional development session. And while she's only been in the teaching profession for a couple of years, she has oh so much wisdom and experience for us to learn from.

When I work directly with students in different districts, I see how these contexts shape education. Each classroom, each school, each community has its own feel, its own challenges, and its own strengths. Seeing this work happen across so many locations has taught me that what works in one place might need to be adjusted for another, but the BISON mentality remains the same.

If I'm being completely honest, the most important part for me and my own growth has been connecting with the mamas in my parent community. These are families trying to navigate the world of special education advocacy. And when I listen to these women talk about their struggles with children who face social and emotional challenges, especially those diagnosed with autism, I understand the educational process in a completely different way. These parents talk about the anxiety of preparing for IEP meetings, how tired they get from advocating for their child's needs, and the constant worry about their child's future. They share the frustration of writing email after email to administrators, trying to get their child's needs met while working through complicated systems.

Understanding the parent perspective has been game-changing. Hearing about the sleepless nights spent wondering if a child will find acceptance, the heartbreak of watching a child struggle socially—it adds layers of meaning to every educational decision. These parents bring intimate knowledge of their children's lives outside school walls. They see the meltdowns after difficult days, the joy when something finally clicks, and the daily victories that often go unnoticed in formal assessments.

This parent perspective also illuminates the administration's role from a different angle. When parents share their experiences of advocating through endless email chains, of feeling unheard in meetings, or of celebrating when an administrator finally "gets it," this reveals how crucial it is for leaders to understand the emotional weight that families carry. The parent community has taught me that behind every IEP meeting, every accommodation request, and every advocacy effort is a family trying to ensure their child has the best possible chance at success and belonging.

In leadership, seeking these diverse perspectives means valuing what others bring to the table and recognizing that we don't have all the answers and we're not meant to. My role as an educator and leader requires me to remain open to new ideas, whether they come from a colleague teaching in a rural community, a parent advocating for their child, or a fellow educator who has navigated a crisis. When you bring together teachers from different geographical contexts, parents with lived experience, and professionals who have faced various challenges, you create a collective wisdom that can better address the complex needs of students.

The value of perspective-taking is that it allows us to better empathize with others, leading to more meaningful connections. When I reach out to understand how different communities support their students, or when I listen to parents share their advocacy journeys, I'm not just seeking information; I'm seeking understanding. The dialogue and collaboration help me gain a deeper understanding of the multifaceted nature of educational support, empowering me to be a more effective leader. And you can have that too.

Ultimately, perspective-taking is about breaking down the walls that separate our personal and professional lives, our different geographical contexts, and our various roles in a child's life. It's about recognizing that our personal struggles, our regional experiences, and our unique challenges shape who we are as educators, leaders, and advocates. When we embrace the diverse perspectives of those around us, we create a stronger, more connected community. This is the foundation of true collaboration. Everyone is valued, and we can collectively grow and support each other in our shared mission of helping students succeed.

CREATE COLLABORATIVE ENVIRONMENTS

In many learning environments, particularly among adults, there's often an underlying sense of competition. Whether it's within friend groups, among colleagues, or even between leaders, there's a constant push to go first, to be right, to have the best idea, or to be seen as the most successful. But what if instead of competing, we intentionally focused on collaborating? True community thrives on connection, not competition.

When I worked alongside the speech pathologist to support educators across our school district, we weren't competing for control or for recognition; we were collaborating. You should also know that she truly did not want to stand on a stage and deliver information to teachers. #NotHerJam—and I might have forced her. But our genuine admiration for each other and our desire to help others anchored us to our mission and purpose without competition.

As educators, we often face the temptation to bring in the next "best thing" or the latest trendy method we learned about at a conference. We hope to be seen as the one with the solution. But that wasn't my goal. I wasn't looking to one-up my colleagues. Instead, I had found something that could support me in the classroom, and I knew it could also help them. I wasn't trying to prove that I had the better approach. The speech pathologist and I were simply working together, bringing our knowledge as educators and specialists into the classroom for the benefit of students and teachers. Our collaboration wasn't about having all the answers; it was about being open to what we both brought to the table and learning from each other.

We focused on finding what was best for the students, as well as what supported us as adults in the process. This approach allowed us to create a space where both of our professional perspectives were valued. We saw eye to eye, both of us committed to doing what was best for the kids.

True collaboration happens when we remove the fear of judgment and competition and instead focus on creating an environment where everyone's ideas and experiences are honored. However, too often in educational settings, competition creeps in even when we're trying to collaborate. We've all seen it. Those subtle signs that people are trying to outdo each other or prove their worth. When collaboration becomes a comparison game, it defeats the purpose. For example, we might be tempted to compare our classroom management techniques, lesson plans, or student outcomes with those of our colleagues. The focus shifts from shared goals to who's doing it "right." This, my friends, is ego getting in the way. And this dynamic can leave teachers feeling unsupported or reluctant to share ideas for fear of judgment.

Instead, we need to create a collaborative environment where educators feel safe enough to ask for help, share resources freely, and contribute without the fear of competition. The key is to cultivate trust and vulnerability. This means fostering a culture where everyone feels their contribution matters. In my experience, when we collaborate with a heart-centered approach, genuinely seeking to support each other and our students, everyone benefits. It's not about being the best but about being the most supportive.

The community you build with your colleagues should feel like a sanctuary. A place where each person's contribution is valued, where differing perspectives are not only welcomed but celebrated, where we leave our egos at the door, and where collaboration happens freely without the shadow of competition. In this space, no one is vying for the spotlight because the collective goal is bigger than individual recognition. By lifting each other up, we create a stronger, more supportive community. This is where impact and a culture shift can begin.

SELEBRATE COLLECTIVE WINS

One of my favorite summers as a dance teacher was when I had a musical theater and jazz dance camp at a studio I was working in. At the very end of the week, I choreographed a dance to the song "We're All in This Together" from *High School Musical*. When I think back to that time, and especially after everything we experienced with the pandemic, I realize just how powerful that message is in every aspect of life, especially in education. Whether it's within a family unit, a classroom, or a school, the truth is simple: We are not meant to do this work alone. We truly are all in this together. We are meant to lean on each other, support one another, and celebrate the collective wins that come from collaboration. We need to embrace the unique strengths and contributions of every individual, recognizing how each person plays a vital role in overall success.

True collaboration is not about singling out one person's achievements. It's about celebrating the entire team and acknowledging how everyone's efforts brought about the win. This might mean recognizing the quiet colleague who was always there to listen and offer support, or the one who helped to keep things calm when stress levels were high. It could be the person who always brings positive energy, the one who thinks outside the box, or the one who keeps everyone on track with structure and organization. All these contributions, big and small, are essential to the success of the group. When we intentionally highlight collective achievements rather than focus on individual accolades, we foster a culture of shared pride and belonging.

I've seen this in action at a school where the strengths of every educator were celebrated. The principal was filled with energy and enthusiasm, elevating every pep rally and assembly. He even sent out a video every Monday that set the tone for the week. The excitement could be felt throughout the school. New teachers continuously stepped in with fresh energy, ready to take on challenges and grow, while seasoned educators, who had witnessed the pendulum of education swing back and forth, offered wisdom and support to help navigate new initiatives and professional development opportunities. When needs arose, whether they were visual support for students in the cafeteria or a new system to improve schoolwide communication, a team of teachers was ready to step in. Some took on the tech aspect, others captured the visuals, and all ensured that students were supported. Everyone spoke the same language, working toward a common goal. These were educators who weren't just showing up for the job. They were showing up for the kids, for each other, and for the shared mission of making a lasting impact.

After a few years of working together to build this culture across the campus, my team and I were able to go inside other classrooms and see this magic happening, and it literally brought groups of teachers to tears. When we had conversations afterward, the teachers across this site told us they were just so grateful to have this group of colleagues who understood they were all truly in it together. Students were engaged, thriving, and supported in ways that felt seamless and intentional. What was happening in those classrooms wasn't by chance. It was the result of a fully aligned staff all speaking the same language and using their unique gifts to support kids in meaningful ways. There was no competition, no ego. Just a collective belief in the power of collaboration and the impact that can be made together.

I know those educators are still doing amazing things, and I know that because they celebrate one another. They are such team players. They do leave their egos at the door, and even when district priorities shift or support changes, they remain committed to the work because they know it matters. They asked me how they could sustain their progress and continue to grow on their own, and my answer was simple: They already have everything they need because they're all on the same page. What they've built is so special, and they get to continue moving this work forward.

You see, when we operate in silos, we miss out on the opportunity to truly celebrate collective wins. When everyone feels seen and appreciated for their individual contributions, it fosters an environment of trust, collaboration, and mutual respect. By celebrating these collective wins, we inspire others to see the value in working together and to recognize that in the end, it's the teamwork that leads to the greatest success.

This approach doesn't just apply to school staff. It's also reflected in the classroom with students. When we acknowledge and celebrate the diverse strengths of our students, whether it's their creativity, kindness, problem-solving abilities, or leadership, we're teaching them the value of working together and supporting one another. This sense of unity, fostered by celebrating collective wins, becomes the foundation for an environment where everyone feels valued, where success is a shared achievement, and where we can all grow.

LEAD WITH FEELING

As leaders, one of the most important things we can do is figure out how we want our schools, our classrooms, and our teams to feel. When I think about how the principals I work with approach leadership, I realize that some really take their time to envision the atmosphere they want to create for their schools. They don't just want a high-performing school; they want a school where people feel supported, valued, and empowered. They don't just focus on the what: the curriculum, the test scores, or the systems. Instead, they also focus on the how: how we make people feel, how we communicate, and how we connect to the families in the community. Some principals intentionally take action toward that vision, creating environments where everyone can feel successful.

As teachers, we get to do the same. We can think about how we want to feel at school, how we want to feel with our grade-level teams, with our colleagues, and in our own classrooms. It's within our power to intentionally take action toward creating the environment we desire. But there's a catch to this. To lead with feeling, we have to listen. We have to listen to ourselves, to our colleagues, and to our students. Only when we truly understand the emotions and needs of those around us can we take meaningful steps toward creating the environment we envision.

Leading with empathy is the secret here. It requires us to recognize that teachers are not superheroes. They are human. They are navigating life just like everyone else, carrying unseen burdens that impact how they show up each day. Some of our best educators and leaders are neurodivergent themselves. *They* may have ADHD, anxiety, or other challenges, diagnosed or undiagnosed, that affect how they process information, manage executive functioning skills, and regulate their emotions. Yet we often expect them to seamlessly support students with these same struggles, without offering the same understanding or grace for their own challenges.

I saw this play out recently with one of my teachers. She came to me frustrated with her administrator. This administrator is incredibly creative and passionate, bringing so many innovative ideas to their school. But sometimes balls get dropped, questions go unanswered, and follow-through can be inconsistent. For a teacher who thrives on order, planning, and predictability, this can be incredibly difficult to deal with.

When this teacher vented to me, I gently asked, "Do you think maybe their brain just thinks differently? Maybe they really struggle with planning ahead and execution in the same way some of our students do?"

And it was in that moment that I heard something shift in her. That recognition. Suddenly, she wasn't seeing this administrator through the lens of what they lacked but through the lens of their gifts and talents. She began to understand that just like our students, this person's brain might be wired differently, and instead of judgment, she could approach the situation with empathy and find ways to work with those differences rather than against them.

The greatest lesson I've learned in both teaching and coaching is that there is always more beneath the surface. Just like with students, we must look beyond behavior and dig deeper to understand the why. People are the way they are for a reason. They have experiences, struggles, and challenges that shape them. Instead of assuming everyone can regulate, plan ahead, and execute flawlessly, we need to recognize that for some, breaking tasks down, prioritizing, or even just making it through the day can be incredibly difficult. Some struggle with seeing the end goal and working backwards, whether that's planning lessons, managing time, or navigating professional expectations.

What's interesting is that we often extend more understanding to students than we do to the adults in the room. We instinctively seek to understand kids' challenges, but when it comes to our colleagues, or our administration, we sometimes forget that they, too, need support, grace, and empathy. Leading with empathy means truly seeing the person behind the role. Acknowledging their humanity, listening to their experiences, and offering the same compassion we would want extended to us. When we create environments where adults feel safe, understood, and valued, that sense of security trickles down to the students. Because when teachers feel supported, they show up as their best selves for their students, for each other, and for the work that truly matters.

WELCOME VULNERABILITY

Vulnerability isn't weakness. It's an invitation for connection. And as leaders, we must model this vulnerability. A principal must be vulnerable too. It's important to recognize that we don't have to have all the answers to all the things all the time, and it's okay not to. We need to be open to being vulnerable and invite others to do the same.

Sometimes, we put up walls because it feels safer, especially when we're stepping into the unknown. But that's the very place where growth happens. Vulnerability means acknowledging that things might fail, but that's what it's all about. We have to take action. Every action teaches us something. Even when something doesn't work, we can step back and ask, "What didn't work? Why? And how can I tweak it to keep moving toward success?" The key there is *when* something doesn't work. Success will come, but only if we keep pulling ourselves forward.

I remember this one moment that solidified something for me as a teacher. I was friends with some of our families on Facebook. You know, they'd sent me friend requests and I'd accepted them because why not? These are people I care about, and their children are in my care for more hours in the day than they're with their own parents. I'm the caretaker. Honestly, I'm teaching them, but I'm also taking care of these babies. It's heartfelt work. That's why I think it's so important in education for everyone to open up and be real with each other. Kids need to feel safe making mistakes and learning. Teachers need to feel safe being human. Parents need to feel safe sharing their concerns and celebrations.

Well, a colleague overheard me talking about a series of Facebook messages I'd exchanged with some of the parents from my class. She just looked at me like I was weird. She couldn't wrap her head around why I would even acknowledge what they'd posted, like there needed to be this hard boundary or wall up when it came to parent and teacher relationships. To her, it was absolutely astonishing that I would be Facebook friends with families at all. How dare I? And that's when I had my big realization: One of my greatest gifts is my ability to connect. Letting people in and showing them that I see and care about them beyond the classroom builds genuine relationships. Families, students, and colleagues don't just want a teacher or leader who follows a script. They want someone who understands them, listens to them, and is willing to be real with them. Am I telling you all to become friends on Facebook with all the families across your campus? Absolutely not.

But there is a sense of openness that we all must cultivate in order to welcome vulnerability.

The same is true within my coaching community. Some of the deepest connections I've built with educators across the country have come from being honest about my own struggles, whether as a mom, a wife, or a teacher navigating self-doubt. When we open up about our shared experiences, anxieties, and challenges, we realize that we are not alone. Vulnerability has a way of dissolving barriers and bringing people closer together. It allows us to move beyond surface-level conversations and into the real, raw spaces where support and growth happen.

I see this even in my posts on Instagram. The ones that get the most likes and shares are always the vulnerable ones. When I found out I was going to be publishing this book, I broke down in tears and posted a video, a reel of me crying. Crying as I was telling my friends, crying as I was telling my spouse. That post went wild. People could relate. Maybe not to the opportunity to write their own book, but definitely to a time in their lives when something so incredible, so special, so out of this world happened to them and brought them to tears. And instead of us all shoving these things down and pretending nothing can crack us open, we need to talk. It helps people feel less alone in their own struggles. We need to welcome vulnerability, with a big ole welcome mat. It's scary to lay yourself out there. It can feel overwhelming. But it's in these moments that people really do connect.

Now I'm not telling you to start posting all your most vulnerable moments on the 'Gram or anything. But to show up as your true self, you need to open up first. I know it can be difficult for some of us. But when you allow those walls to come down, and people start learning more about the experiences that make you *you*, it enables this unbelievable sense of deep connection.

On the other hand, when walls go up and vulnerability is absent, a culture of judgment and fear emerges. Educators who don't feel safe in their schools often find themselves constantly scrutinized by administrators or colleagues in positions of power. This makes them hesitant to take risks or show up as their true selves. When people feel judged rather than supported, they begin to shut down, and their willingness to collaborate, innovate, and grow disappears.

In these environments, fear stifles progress, and educators operate in survival mode rather than thrive as professionals. But real change in education doesn't come from fear; it comes from trust, connection, and the willingness to be open with one another. If we want to create schools where both teachers and students flourish, we must build a culture where authenticity is valued, struggles are acknowledged, and everyone feels safe enough to grow.

Vulnerability is not about oversharing or disregarding boundaries but about showing up as your true self and allowing others to do the same. It's about creating spaces where people feel safe to be honest about their challenges and confident in seeking support. The strongest communities aren't built on perfection or high test scores. They are built on authenticity, trust, and the understanding that we are all in this together. There's that song again!

— CHAPTER 9 —

Building TRUST

Our students don't just need better discipline or more consequences. They need something different. Earlier in this book, I told you how one of my clients said something that stuck with me: "They just don't know how to do school." Let me reiterate that they were right. Some of our kids have lagging skills, and others are lacking school skills entirely.

So what do we do? Do we punish the bad behavior out of them? Shame the good behavior *into* them? Have them sit inside during recess and "teach into" what's missing? Is that really how we're going to move forward in education? Is that what we want to model for the next generation of teachers? I think not. In fact, I'd bet that if you're reading this, you're searching for a better way.

Because here's where we can make a shift. We need each other. We need reminders that we're not alone. We need support, not more bullet points or another icebreaker. We need to build relationships that nurture us. Safety doesn't come from a curriculum book or a PD slide deck. It comes from human connection and mutual support. It's about how we feel, and that begins with leading with vulnerability and empathy. Some of us don't know how to show up for others. But it's never too late to start. We can't convince everyone around us that they need to, but we can control how we show up.

The question isn't what's wrong with these kids. And the answer is not to take away all the technology around them. The solution is figuring out how we shift as educators and parents in a world where technology is constantly advancing. How do we help our students build the neural pathways necessary for growth when the world around them is changing so quickly?

This is the work. This is what we have to figure out together. And we can't do it by punishing kids. The goal isn't control. It isn't about compliance. It's about empowerment. It's about embedding strategies that actually work. Ones that build trust instead of fear. Our job isn't to fix kids. It's to teach them.

Dr. Ross Greene says it best: "Kids do well if they can." But so many schools still operate under the mindset that kids do well if they want to. And that fundamental difference changes everything. When a student struggles, traditional discipline asks why they won't just behave. But the truth is that it's rarely about *won't*. It's about *can't yet*.

If a student doesn't know how to read, we teach them. If they don't know how to multiply, we teach them. So why, when they struggle with emotional regulation, do we assume punishment will "fix" it? We have to shift. We have to be the educators who recognize that behavior is communication. That support, not control, is what truly changes outcomes.

BE INTENTIONAL BY *building trust* SO OTHERS NOTICE A CULTURE OF EMPOWERMENT, NOT CONTROL.

When we focus on empowerment rather than punishment, on support rather than isolation, we stop working against each other and start working together. It's about leading with heart and creating a culture of trust and connection, not control and compliance. And that's the future of education we all deserve.

The truth is that a lot of the dysfunction we see in schools doesn't start in the classroom. It starts in the systems. So often, leadership, whether at the district level or school site, is driven by a desire to control outcomes. But control isn't leadership. When decisions are made from a place of fear or pressure, the result is micromanagement, top-down mandates, and a culture where trust is replaced by compliance. And here's what that creates: educators who are walking on eggshells, afraid to try something new, afraid to speak up, and constantly second-guessing themselves.

When you feel controlled, your instinct is to try and control something, anything, in return. That's where the ripple effect begins. Leaders try to control teachers. Teachers try to control students. Students try to control their environment in the only ways they know how. That is often through behavior that challenges us. Around and around we go. It becomes a cycle of power struggles instead of a system rooted in purpose and connection. No one feels heard. No one feels safe. And worst of all? No one grows.

But when we shift from control to trust, everything changes. When leaders lead with intention and empathy, they build connections instead of compliance. When teachers feel trusted, they're empowered to innovate, reflect, and collaborate. And when students are met with safety instead of shame, they begin to regulate, connect, and grow. That's the real culture shift, and it starts with intentionally choosing empowerment over control, even when it feels messy or uncertain. Because trust isn't just the foundation of good relationships; it's the foundation of sustainable change.

BECOME THE BISON

START WITH EMPATHY

True leadership in education starts with empathy. And don't confuse sympathy with empathy. Sympathy is feeling sorry for someone, looking at their situation from the outside and offering pity. I can't stand people pitying me. Empathy is different. It's stepping into someone's shoes, feeling what they feel, and truly understanding their experience from their perspective. Sympathy keeps distance. Empathy creates connection.

As an administrator, you have the power to shape the culture of your school, not just through policies and procedures but through the way you engage with and support your teachers and staff. Leading with empathy means intentionally seeking to understand the unique challenges, strengths, and experiences of the educators and families in your community. It's about understanding their perspective, meeting them where they are, and acknowledging their humanity.

When I work with educators, I understand the weight they carry in managing challenging student behaviors. It's not about offering surface-level advice. It's about seeing the difficulty in their work and recognizing the emotional strain they're under. It means building trust so others notice your commitment to supporting them. When we lead with empathy, we aren't rushing to fix things with quick solutions; we're listening first, offering validation, and empowering people to act with confidence in the systems we've created together.

When I meet with district leadership about supporting their teachers, I emphasize that educators need more than just strategies. They need individualized coaching and genuine support. Recently, I explained to a group of district leaders that their teachers were asking for someone to come alongside them, to understand their unique classroom dynamics, and to provide tailored guidance through both one-on-one and small-group coaching. However, the team immediately dismissed this approach, insisting that teachers "just need strategies" and that if I couldn't deliver quick, surface-level solutions, they weren't interested in working together.

This response perfectly illustrates the problem. Rather than listening to what teachers needed, this district was rushing toward Band-Aid fixes. True support means taking time to understand each teacher as a person, learning how their classroom operates, and then collaboratively developing next steps that are individualized and meaningful. It's not about implementing generic strategies. It's about building relationships and creating solutions together that address the root of the challenges teachers face.

The same principle applies when working with families. Parents need to feel heard. They need to feel that we understand the unique challenges their children are facing. When we approach families with empathy, we acknowledge the struggles they're experiencing and recognize that *their* role is just as challenging as the educator's. It's important not to offer judgment but instead to ask, "How can I support you?" And it's critical to genuinely listen to their response. Parents, just like students and teachers, are doing the best they can with the tools they have. As leaders, our role is to help them access the support they need, not criticize them for what they lack.

Teachers need to hear that their efforts are seen, that the work is hard, and that we are in this together. Empathy doesn't just happen in moments of crisis. It's about building a culture of understanding and empowerment every day. When administrators lead with empathy, they set the tone for the entire school. They create an environment where teachers feel they can be honest about their struggles, where students feel understood rather than punished, and where families feel like valued partners, not outsiders. It's about recognizing that everyone, no matter their role, is part of the same community, the same herd. Together, we can face any storm that comes our way.

Schools thrive when leaders prioritize connection over compliance, understanding over assumption, and support over control. Leading with empathy isn't just a nice thing to do; it's the foundation for a strong, empowered school community. The BISON mentality—*being intentional so others notice*—starts here, with the foundation of empathy. Because when we lead with empathy, we make space for those around us to thrive, and in turn, they lead with empathy themselves. It's not about being kind to one another but about showing one another empathy through kindness. And together, through these actions, we make a powerful herd that can face any challenge head-on.

EMPOWER CHOICE AND AUTONOMY

Empowering choice and autonomy is crucial to creating an environment where students, teachers, and families feel capable. For administrators or leaders, this means fostering an atmosphere where educators have the freedom to make decisions about their classrooms while feeling supported in their growth. Empowerment comes not from control but from giving educators the space to lead in ways that align with their strengths and passions. When teachers feel trusted, they are more likely to innovate and feel ownership over their work, which ultimately reflects in the classroom and the experiences of their students.

In the classroom, empowering students with autonomy goes far beyond offering a simple choice board. It's not just about letting students pick between writing a report, building a model, or creating a slide deck presentation. It's about teaching them the critical thinking, decision-making, and self-regulation skills they need to navigate those choices successfully. When educators take the time to build these foundational skills, students learn how to advocate for themselves, manage their time, and take ownership of their learning.

For example, instead of saying, "Here are your options, choose one," a teacher might guide students by asking, "What do you think will challenge you the most? Which option will allow you to show your strengths? Think about how much time we have to get this project done, what your schedule looks like outside of class, and then decide which option is the best for you." This intentional scaffolding allows students to step into their independence with confidence rather than uncertainty. True autonomy is not about giving kids unlimited choices but equipping them with the skills to make the right ones.

For students who are struggling with behavior or attention, empowering choice also means helping them understand what's behind their actions. The principle that kids do well if they *can* definitely applies here. If a student is acting out, it's often because they lack the tools or skills to manage their needs. For example, if a student is hungry and acting out as a result, it's important to allow them to eat a snack before rejoining class. Novel idea, right? But you've first got to figure out if hunger is the reason behind their actions. Forcing them to engage when their basic needs aren't met only increases frustration and dysregulation. By addressing the root cause of their behavior, whether physical, emotional, or developmental, we give kids the autonomy to solve their own problems, leading to better outcomes and less resistance.

The same approach applies at home. Often, parents feel the instinct to control a child's behavior when things go wrong, whether it's through punishment or consequences. But instead of focusing on what went wrong, it's more powerful to focus on why it went wrong. If a child is struggling to complete chores, it's important to understand what barriers they're facing. Are they struggling with time management? Do they understand what the task is? Are they overwhelmed by how many steps are involved? A child struggling with homework may not be lazy; they may not know how to break down the task or where to start. When parents take the time to teach these skills, they empower their children to be more independent and capable in the future. This is executive functioning, folks. These are the skills that we all need to be successful. Not just at school with projects. Not just at home with chores. But in life.

When we focus on empowering others with choice and autonomy, we create a culture of trust and responsibility. Students who understand their own needs and are empowered to make choices will develop into more self-sufficient and capable individuals. Teachers who feel supported and trusted are more likely to take risks, try new approaches, and create a learning environment where students can thrive. And when parents focus on understanding their child's needs and empowering them with skills to navigate challenges, they cultivate a foundation of confidence and independence. True empowerment is not about simply offering choices. It's about helping others build the skills and confidence they need to make informed, effective decisions for themselves.

SELEBRATE EFFORT AND PROGRESS

In schools, the focus is often on end results. Administrators are fixated on test scores, data points, and final achievements. Teachers are too. But true progress isn't always about hitting a specific number. It's about recognizing and celebrating the small, daily victories that pave the way for meaningful change. Leaders who value effort and progress, rather than just final outcomes, create a culture of resilience and growth. When educators and students feel their efforts are noticed, no matter how small, it fosters an environment where continuous learning grows. Instead of focusing only on how much further a student or teacher has to go, effective leaders celebrate those incremental steps. A student who grasps a concept a little more clearly today. A teacher who implements a new strategy multiple times throughout the day instead of just once. That's growth. These moments deserve recognition because they reflect forward momentum. And *that* is heading into the storm.

I talk to teachers every single day about how they feel regarding certain things in the classroom. Even the smallest wins are wins. Maybe they turned off the lights to create a calmer mood in their classroom after lunch, or perhaps they front-loaded before and after recess to support their students' transitions. These small, consistent actions can make a significant difference in the classroom culture, and celebrating that effort is key.

Too often, teachers feel they're expected to do more without acknowledgment of the progress they've made. But celebrating those efforts helps them feel supported and valued. For example, if a teacher is working to support students with self-regulation, recognizing those small shifts helps build a culture where effort and progress are recognized and celebrated. Maybe a student who usually blurts something out can hold their thoughts a little longer. Perhaps a child with attention challenges can limit the number of open tabs on their Chromebook. Even when a student who typically disengages smiles, makes eye contact, or walks into class with their head up—these moments matter. The social and emotional work teachers are doing is not only making a difference, it's inspiring everyone around them to keep going.

The same philosophy applies to students. Celebrating the learning that's taking place, no matter how small it might seem, is critical in transforming the culture of a classroom. Maybe a student who usually shuts down when faced with a challenge was willing to try again or ask for help. Maybe they completed part of their classwork independently when they typically avoid it altogether. Or perhaps they communicated their frustration instead of acting out. These small steps are worth celebrating because they reinforce the idea that learning is a process. By recognizing these efforts, teachers and parents continue to create environments where children feel valued and motivated to keep going too. And in a world where student motivation is sometimes lacking, this is the missing piece.

Growth takes time, and the path is rarely straight. It's not about waiting for the finish line. It's about celebrating every small step along the way. When we celebrate effort and progress, we not only create a culture of encouragement and motivation, but we also remind ourselves that even the smallest actions add up to meaningful growth. That's what being a BISON is all about. Moving forward together, with purpose, persistence, and the belief that progress, no matter how small, is always worth celebrating—or SELebrating!

— CHAPTER 10 —

You Are an INSPIRATION

I never wanted to leave my classroom. Ever. It was my happy place. I loved working with kids—the tricky ones, the funny ones, the sweet ones, the quiet ones, and especially the ones who challenged me. To this day, those kids are still my favorite. I could have stayed there forever, content in my little piece of pineapple paradise, but there was this tug inside me that was pulling me in a different direction.

There was a time when I kept that feeling to myself just to avoid an eye roll, an awkward stare, or even worse, the quiet. As teachers, most of us don't get it when one of our own decides that they want to do something bigger, something untapped, something that will help make more of an impact. So I'd close the door to my classroom and live on my own little island. But when I started realizing how much work needed to be done to share the amazingness of SEL with other educators and administrators, I knew it meant leaving my pineapple paradise behind. My classroom chapter was ending, but I faced an exciting new beginning.

When you're ready to expand your SEL impact beyond your own four walls, your work will look different. My role evolved from class-room teacher to district-level support, then to edupreneur, speaker, coach, podcaster, and now author. And everything I learned along the way can guide you too.

My first steps were simple but intentional. As a district Teacher on Special Assignment, I helped create an SEL academy for teachers with representatives from across our school district who elected to join. These were teachers who were all in, who were invested in the work, but they also knew they needed to be consistent. They knew they needed to actually take action because we were going to talk about it the next time we met. They didn't have homework, but they definitely knew that I was going to ask them what was going on in their classrooms—and within themselves.

I kind of flipped the script on PD also. I didn't want to just make a slide deck. I didn't want to spend my time sitting behind a desk at a district office. It was more productive, more impactful, for me to be in the classroom working alongside teachers and getting to know what was really going on. That way, when we did meet, I knew exactly what I wanted to talk about and what we, as a collective, needed to do.

Next, I developed a social-emotional learning road map and brought it to life on a website that housed "what, why, and how" resources for teachers. This became our hub of connection, a place where I could walk into any classroom and immediately pull up a monthly focus as well as language that educators could use in the classroom, anchor chart ideas, visuals, and other resources. Then I would leave these behind so teachers could support themselves in their next steps. (With my business, Teaching Inside Out, I help schools and school districts to create their own hub and resources.)

The website became more than just a resource hub. It was like our very own professional learning and teacher store all in one place. Educators could grab and go all year long. We housed everything along with clear road maps, nonnegotiables, and systems that outlined who we are and why we do things. It was sustainable because it was systematic.

Through data, we discovered that teachers needed more intentional in-person, in-classroom support—not just someone to pull out a kid when they were acting up. Our behavior support aides weren't assigned to schools for random read-alouds or help wrangling students. Instead, they were strategically placed at specific school sites with chunked-out schedules to support groups of children. They were working alongside teachers to ease transitions, guide new systems, and model vocabulary and phrases. Our focus was to get ahead of the behaviors. To model, guide, and teach into the skills that were lagging while creating a sense of calm and control in the classroom.

But here's what made it really powerful. Once a month, these aides were pulled out to work alongside me. I would model for them in classrooms, and then they would coach each other and work with students back in their own classrooms. We would talk about the strategies that were working and what we might add to our toolbox. This is why they were able to learn so much so quickly. I wasn't just throwing them to the wolves. I was showing them how to get out there, learn, and grow while reminding them that I'd be walking alongside them every step of the way. They knew they'd continue to get feedback on things that were working, on ways they could support themselves, and on methods to help the kids and the teachers. It was like professional development, live and in action.

You know who these people were? The academy members, the teachers we trained, the behavior support aides? They were part of my herd. We were part of each other's herd. We had, gratefully, thankfully, found each other, and we could head into the storm together.

BE INTENTIONAL BY *expanding* WITH YOUR COMMUNITY SO OTHERS NOTICE WHAT'S POSSIBLE, NOT JUST WHAT'S EXPECTED.

In the pages that follow, you'll discover how to identify, build, and nurture your own herd. Because the truth is that this work isn't meant to be done alone. Whether you're still in your classroom or ready to expand your impact, you need your people, and they need you. We're going to talk about how to find them, keep them, and how we can continue to grow together.

BECOME THE BISON

RUN WITH YOUR HERD

One of the first big conferences I was asked to speak at was in San Francisco. I had been posting all over social media that I was going to be driving from SoCal with my husband as my chauffeur and that I'd be speaking about social-emotional learning in the classroom and how to sustain it across a district. Some people from New York reached out and said that their group of school experts and specialists was going to be there. Fast-forward to the conference and I finally got to meet my virtual friends in person. It was amazing. We posed for pictures, chatted about their next steps, and continued to talk for weeks after through Instagram.

Not long after the conference, one of my newfound New Yorker friends messaged me and asked if we could FaceTime so she could pick my brain some more and show me the work that they had done at their site. So we chatted. I learned what they were doing, asked questions, and gave advice and next steps. When I got off the phone, I knew I needed more of *that* in my life. I remember talking to a colleague at the time about what had just happened. She looked at me like I had completely lost my shit. Why in the world would I spend time talking to people in New York? Why wasn't I sitting behind my desk pumping out slide decks and presentations? And how could I possibly want to do more of what I'd just done?

Well, I saw this educator in New York as someone who was expanding me. She made me feel like I could do more. She made me feel like there was more that I *needed* to do. We were supporting each other and strengthening our herd, and you need people like this in your life.

So you're probably thinking, "That's cool, Kim, but what if I don't give keynotes at conferences or have thousands of Instagram followers? How do I meet *my* people?"

I have connected with so many life-giving, soul-supporting humans by taking a leap of faith and sliding into their DMs. My favorite authors? Yup. My favorite educators? Absolutely. Buy a ticket to fly out and meet them in person? Oh, I've definitely done that—and stayed at their houses! Fast-forward to today, and they're part of my inner circle. They come to my events, they drop anything to hop on a quick call or send a voice note, and three of them even started a podcast for my ViBE EDU conference without blinking an eye. But you've got to start somewhere. You've got to take that small step to find and connect with your people. In isolation, there is burnout. And I don't want that for you. You don't want that for yourself. Your herd is your lifeline.

At this very moment in your teaching career, you are somewhere in the pack of teachers all running in the same direction: You're trying to get to the end of the school year alongside your students and colleagues, and no matter where you are in that pack, you are running with people. You're also inspiring others, and you most definitely need to seek out people to expand you.

But who are you running with? Who are the people that you collaborate with daily? Who are the people you eat lunch with, plan with, go to happy hour with? Who are your people in your inner circle right now? These are the people I want you to think about first.

Maybe you don't go to happy hour. Maybe you like to eat lunch alone. To help you figure out who the people you're running with are, you can ask yourself the following questions: Who are the people making you feel safe and seen? The people who make your nervous system feel calm and easy? You don't ever have to fear that they will judge you, your thoughts, your ideas, or your actions. You know that you'll only get feedback, not a sense of failure. These are the people who will go to bat for you, even in rooms you're not physically present in. Use that analogy, and you'll quickly realize who these people are. *Those* are the people you're running with, and you better be choosy. Because you get to be. This is you protecting your peace right here.

When you choose who you're running with, a shift happens. It's this united front that we create. It's this closeness and bond like no other. And nothing will break it. There's an absence of competition and competitiveness. No one is trying to one-up the other. They're only there to guide, support, listen, and help you stay in your lane with your head held high and your feet on the ground.

For some of us, if we're lucky enough, these people exist at our school sites and across our district. And for others, we get to go in search of them across the country. Read that again. You get to find them. And while we're searching, because we all are, I want you to remember this: You must find *your* people. And once you find them, hold on to them, love on them, and don't let go. If they're truly the people you're meant to be running with, they'll do the same right back to you because they've noticed the same thing in you. They need you running alongside them just as much as you need them running alongside you. And man, that is such a good feeling.

COLLABORATE WITHOUT COMPETITION

As an educator, you need a community that collaborates, guides, and supports you, without competition. You need to immerse yourself in the company of educators who are just like you, who understand what you're going through, who lift you up, who breathe life into you and your work, and who see you for the brilliant educator you are. Because when you're surrounded with mentors and educators who are just like you, you feel empowered. And when you're empowered with the tools, strategies, systems, and language that transforms your classroom—and when the people in your innermost circle continuously love on you and gently guide you—you start to feel the support you need to continue the work that you were born to do. And you'll do it well. These are the people who are expanding you. You need them running with you. You need to be choosy about who you run with, and you get to be choosy with the mentors who are pulling you forward too.

Some of us, even as adults, don't understand how to show up for people. Some don't know how to show up consistently or how to create true, loving, supportive, long-lasting relationships with the people around us. But there are practices you can learn to become better at supporting others.

If you were to evaluate yourself, right now, what would you say? Are you able to pour into others? Are you able to see what someone else needs and adapt your behavior to support those needs? Or is it difficult for you? Do you have room to grow? Perspective-taking, truly being able to put yourself in someone else's shoes, is tricky. It's a skill that some of us have practiced for years and take for granted. And for others, it's a skill that may be lagging or even lacking. When it happens, it can unintentionally impact our relationships.

Think of a text message that you recently received from a friend, family member, or colleague that made you pause. One that made you go, "What was that all about? That was off." Or maybe you caught yourself thinking, "I feel like they could have handled that differently."

It doesn't necessarily mean that the sender of the text is unkind or inconsiderate; they might just be struggling with perspective-taking. Maybe they're stressed, or their social and emotional awareness hasn't been intentionally developed. The truth is, this shows up everywhere: in classrooms, in staff meetings, in our homes. Teachers who can't see through the eyes of their students. Administrators who can't step into the experience of their teachers. Parents who can't see through the eyes of the kids—and vice versa. When we build perspective-taking skills, we don't just strengthen empathy, we strengthen connection, communication, and trust.

As educators, some of us think that building relationships is simply what we do. It's what we've been *told* we need to do. We're told at our PDs, shown through our curriculum, and exposed to this idea through Pinterest or TikTok—but there's so much more to it. Common language and systems give you the *how*. They give you the *why*. And if you're born with a brain that makes creating relationships difficult for you, the language and systems guide you on how to do this work effectively—not only so you can build relationships with your students, but so you can build a relationship with yourSELf.

So much of our exhaustion as educators comes from the constant mental chatter. The endless loop of questioning whether we're doing it right, worrying that someone will change everything up on us, wondering if we're doing enough or could be doing more. We carry our students' struggles home with us, replay parent conversations, and second-guess every email we send.

We pour ourselves out all day long for our students, their families, and our colleagues. We problem-solve *their* challenges and celebrate *their* wins. But when the day ends and we're running on empty, we have little left for our own families and friends. And sometimes—most of the time—nothing left for ourselves.

But it's important to note that you need to be intentional about who's expanding you in your herd. Educators need consistent mentorship and connection throughout their career. They need consistent guidance, love, and support from a community of like-minded people. Because sometimes the mentorship role in our schools or districts, or even in state-funded organizations, can feel yucky. It doesn't feel safe. It doesn't feel like you can let your walls down. It feels like you've got to watch your back, like any wrong step you take or small slipup is going to go straight to your administrator—or worse, to your colleagues.

Too many times I've seen and heard from educators across this nation who don't feel supported by the people claiming to be their biggest supporters. Being a mentor isn't just about the title. It takes *work*! You've got to be viewed as a safe person. Colleagues and educators you work with need to feel like they can be vulnerable with you, that they're in a space where they'll receive nonjudgmental feedback.

Educators need mentors who will stand up for them, not tear them down. And it's this consistent love and support that allows teachers to transform. We're superheroes, not superhuman. We're messy, creative, passionate, and sometimes a lot to handle. But that's what makes us perfect for the job of pouring into kids. They need that. They need it messy. They need the creativity. They need the passion. Because guess what? *They* are a lot to handle too!

I'll never forget the day I first heard Taylor's voice. My first-grade team had been called into the principal's office for a conference call at the beginning of the school year. She was about to hire Taylor as our fourth team member because enrollment had gone up and we needed to create another class. I remember sitting in that chair, listening to Taylor's bubbly, energetic voice coming through the speaker, and in that moment, I looked at my teammates and mouthed, "Yep, she's the one."

The very first time I saw Taylor in person, I ran up to her and gave her the biggest hug. I instantly knew just how special our relationship was going to be.

Taylor worked through her induction program to clear her credential, and I had the privilege, the honor, of being her mentor. When my principal suggested we'd be a good fit, I didn't hesitate. "Done. Sign me up. This girl is pure light and gold."

Taylor was the type of teacher who would come into my classroom every single morning. We would both arrive super early because that's just who we are. It filled our cups to have a calm start to the day. She would find me on the floor creating anchor charts, and I would share everything: my teaching points for the day across multiple subjects, the picture books I planned to read, how I was connecting it all, the crafts and writing activities. She would soak it all in and then take it and fly.

But our connection went far beyond teaching. We bonded over our shared love of Disneyland, Frenchies, shopping, drinking champagne, and laughing until our cheeks hurt. We'd put our feet up on Fridays wearing matching socks or shoes or T-shirts, whatever coordinated moment we'd planned that week. Taylor didn't just become my mentee. She became my friend, my *sister*.

She still is today. And now she can walk into any classroom, instantly absorb what's happening, and then take those ideas and run with them in her own beautiful way. It's amazing to watch. But here's what makes it truly beautiful: Creating relationships with kids, with that social-emotional learning piece, comes so naturally to her.

Life has both challenged and propelled Taylor in the most amazing ways. She has a son who was diagnosed with autism, and while she's always had a gift for teaching into lagging social and emotional skills, this experience has transformed her into an even more powerful advocate and educator. She has become her son's voice and has developed deep knowledge and expertise. And she doesn't just advocate for her own child; she's also a voice for all of her students. Because she just gets it. Anyone who walks into her classroom knows it feels magical. She understands how to build relationships, how to speak to kids—especially the ones that challenge her—how to change her tone and tempo based on the energy in the room, and how to give each child what they need to feel seen, supported, and loved. These abilities have always been within her.

And as her mentor, I got to help her fly. I helped her organize her thoughts, showed her how to put all the pieces of curriculum together, and watched her soar. But more than that, I created a safe space where she could talk about the hard things—not just classroom challenges but personal stuff too. She knew she wouldn't be judged, and sometimes she just needed someone to listen. That safety is what allowed her to take risks, ask questions, and grow without fear of doing something wrong.

Yes, it was two years of an "official" mentor and mentee relationship, but it's been almost a decade of this beautiful connection we've created. It's all anchored in safety, and I still get to be that person for her, even from a thousand miles away. Being part of someone's journey like that, running alongside her while also pulling her toward expansion—that's the beauty of mentorship.

After completing induction and clearing her credential, Taylor was chosen to speak at our big colloquium at the end of year 2. She has always excelled in this profession, always stood out from the rest, so it came as no surprise that she was selected to share her story with other new teachers.

In her speech, she said something that has stuck with me for years now: "If you don't have a Kim Gameroz in your life, I really suggest you get one."

Little did I know *that* line would become a driving force in my own journey. Taylor might have been the first teacher I had the honor of mentoring, but she was not the last. She paved the way for all of this: how to create a safe space for connection and collaboration, how to pour into others and watch them become the best versions of themselves. Dare I say, the BISON versions of themselves. The intentional versions.

Because when you have supportive and loving relationships with your students, families, colleagues, administration, and mentors—when you have the emotional intelligence and understanding of how to show up for one another consistently, to huddle with your herd—that is the power of the BISON.

INCLUDE YOUR STUDENTS

Each year, I put together the most beautiful teacher SELebration, called the Bloom. It's honestly the most incredible two-day retreat for the educators and district leaders who are part of my community over at SELebrate Good Times. These are the people who truly exemplify what it means to be a BISON. And each year, I invite my former student Lucie to come and speak. Now a teen, she was only six years old when she came into my classroom and changed me forever.

I usually remind her about the chapter book she wrote in my first-grade class, *The Seasons*. She read it in front of the entire elementary school, wearing hot-pink heart-shaped sunglasses and boots. I joke that she owes her incredible writing talent all to me, her favorite first-grade teacher. Well, only half kidding right there!

This year, we're going even bigger. Lucie's taking the main stage at ViBE EDU, our conference out in Southern California. I always send her a video of me asking her if she's up for it. Her response when I asked this year? "Of course! These teachers need to know how to help kids like me!"

Listen, when Lucie speaks, she doesn't sugarcoat anything. She'll tell you straight up that having autism means her brain works differently, and you know what? She's proud of it. She wrote this poem called "My Special Thing" where she says, "Some people think that my Autism isn't nice at all, but for me? I think it's very beautiful." That right there? That's the kind of perspective that changes everything.

She'll talk to you about her gifts, how she can hear any musical note and tell you exactly what it is, something even her choir teacher can't do. She has this incredible memory and gets amazing grades because of it. But she's also real about the hard stuff. She talks about "rock brain" making it tough to be flexible, and "worry wall" causing anxiety about things like state testing.

And here's what gets me every single time. She remembers being punished for behaviors that were just her brain trying to navigate a world that didn't understand her yet. Standing against the wall at lunch, feeling ashamed and crying because she thought she was helping another kid but the adults saw it as being disruptive. Or getting in trouble for telling a teacher she was being too loud when her sensitive hearing was overwhelmed.

But then she'll tell you about her math teacher who took the time to understand her, who gave the class more time to pack up, who checked in with her. Lucie became Student of the Month in that class. Same kid, different approach, completely different outcome.

When she talks to teachers, Lucie says, "You are bucket fillers, not bucket dippers. Keep on filling those buckets!" And honestly, I get chills, and tears, every time she speaks because she's living proof of what happens when we focus on filling one another up instead of draining and tearing each other down.

If you didn't already get where I was going with this, let me lay it out for you. Lucie is 100 percent a key member of my herd.

But here's the thing about our relationship: She's not just someone I'm mentoring. Yeah, I'm cheering her on and helping her see her gifts, but she's also teaching me things I never knew I needed to learn. She's expanding my heart and my understanding in ways that make me a better educator. That's the beauty of this whole journey we're on together. Some people are running alongside us, some are ahead showing us the way, and some are behind us looking for encouragement. Lucie? She's all of those things to me at different moments, and that's what makes her so special.

And it's not just our incredible *former* students who become BISON. They're already BISON when they begin to do the work with you.

One of my favorite stories is about a fifth-grade teacher who was having a tough time with her students' behavior in PE. Instead of getting frustrated, she brought the class together to talk about it. They discussed the possible reasons why certain behaviors were happening in PE but not in the classroom. Together, they reflected on what might be different about those environments and what they could do about it. Then, before heading off to PE, the teacher had her students set intentional goals—asking them how they were going to show BISON behavior that day. The shift was almost immediate. The PE teacher couldn't believe the difference in the students' behavior and made sure to let that fifth-grade teacher know just how much they noticed.

That is the power of the BISON. Because when you're intentional, other people notice the difference. And what did this teacher do? She SELebrated her students. She gave out a BISON of the Week Award (a bison stuffed animal) that individual students got to display on their desks. And when I came in to visit them, they were beyond excited to show me their prized possession. You guys, fifth graders!

And it doesn't stop there. There are fourth graders who create clothing, hats, and food items out of little pieces of colored, cut, and folded paper for their beloved bison. Middle schoolers are talking about being intentional so others notice—something that brings me to my knees. Primary students are wearing their "brag tags" every Friday and talking about their BISON song they've created with AI. There are classrooms where the MVB (Most Valuable BISON) of the week will wear their class's bison hat, and their teacher takes their picture and displays it on a board titled "Our MVBs!" There are weekly SELebrations where kids sing along to "Celebration" by Kool and the Gang. Classes create cheers and chants when their peers get SELebrated. Man, there are some incredible moments for kids that are being created all across this country. That BISON force is strong, and if you're reading this thinking, "Oh, I've got to get me some of *that*," well then consider this a sign. Your students are just waiting to learn to be intentional and run into the storm along with you.

THINK OF WHO YOU'RE INSPIRING

Who are the people you inspire? These are the people *you* are expanding and who are running behind you. Yes, they're your students and children, but they're also the adults around you. They might be running at a slower pace—maybe they're a brand-new teacher, a classified employee, an aide, or even a student teacher. And they're looking at you like they're saying, "Oh my goodness, I need to soak in this magic so that one day I'll have it all together just like you."

Read that again. Just like *you*. These people are looking to *you* because they think you've got it goin' on! They're inspired by the energy, creativity, or just the way you are around your students. They're wondering how you're able to run as if you're just starting this marathon, and they're looking to you for support and guidance so that they can one day look, feel, teach, and lead just like you.

It can be hard for us to remember this when we're in the thick of things. We get so wrapped up in the race that we sometimes forget there are educators out there who want to expand themselves. But you are inspiring the people around you right this minute. Some of you may not even realize it, but the things you post on your social media, the student work that you put up in the hallways, what you're pinning on your Pinterest boards, the tone of your voice, your ability to organize things, your anchor charts, your ability to take students' work and make it look like a beautiful art piece—all of these things are inspiring people. They're inspiring people in your innermost circle, your family members, your colleagues, the families who walk down the halls of your school, the moms who help out in their child's classroom or sit in the hallways organizing folders or stapling projects. Hell, you are inspiring complete and total strangers when your pictures or videos pop up on Facebook and Instagram. And I've got a secret for you. Some of these people are going to tell you to your face that you are inspiring them, while others will hold it in.

The people who hold it in are the ones you won't ever know you've inspired. These are the people who hang in the shadows, or the ones who silently stalk you on TikTok. They are watching, hanging on every move you make, outfit you wear, project you post, video you create—and they'll never say a word to you. Maybe they're complete strangers. Some of these people you will never meet face-to-face. But you have to remember this: They're out there. I promise you they are.

These people see you, they respect you, they admire the work that you do, and they are cheering for you. They want the absolute best for you. They're your people. They feel genuinely connected to you and what you stand for. They're running that marathon behind you, and they're thinking, "I know I can do this because [your name here] can do this." You must always remember that you are inspiring them. You are intentional in the work that you do, and because of this, they notice. And even if you don't know who they are, these people are part of your herd too.

GET RID OF THE BOX

I hope it's already clear why thinking of your herd is the best way to bring SEL into your classroom. We need support and we need practice to do the hard work of being intentional with ourselves and with our students. But what do most of our school districts do to incorporate SEL? They purchase some sort of boxed curriculum, or they hire another Teacher on Special Assignment to lead, coordinate, or specialize in this work. Depending on the state and school district, they might even take teachers out of the classroom and put them into these positions. This is meant to support our students and teachers (under the guise of intervention), but instead of feeling supported, the teachers left behind in the classroom now feel inundated. They're still working with twenty-five to thirty-six students, or, if they're secondary teachers, they still have multiple periods and over a hundred students all day long. And now they have a colleague telling them what they're not doing and what they need to do? That sure doesn't feel like support in the slightest.

Believe me, I get it. If you're selected to be in one of these SEL positions, it sure does feel like you're creating an impact. You really are working so hard. But to the teachers left behind, you're no longer one of them. You're not crawling on the floor, calling the nurse about another lice outbreak, or writing report cards. You're not attending after-school PD or doing parking lot duty. You're different now. You're one more thing that's been added to their plate.

Let's talk about that boxed curriculum for a minute. You know the one. You're flipping through lessons filled with activities and scenarios that bear no connection to your classroom. Nothing feels real. It's all "what if" situations that ask kids to jump into the minds of people they've never met and deal with problems they've never faced.

Here's the thing: For our kids who struggle with perspective-taking, it's incredibly hard to make that leap into someone else's brain, especially when that someone is a fictional character in a made-up scenario. And our kids who *do* know all the right answers? They can tell you exactly what skills and strategies the other kids should be using, but when it's their turn to use those same tools in the heat of the moment, everything falls apart.

That's where the box curriculum comes up short. It's missing the most important ingredient: your actual kids, in your actual classroom, dealing with their actual struggles.

The BISON approach is completely different from this one-and-done mentality. And the beautiful part is you can adopt this approach yourself, not just by hiring my team at Teaching Inside Out (though we'd love to support you!).

Real support looks like having people from the outside meet your teachers exactly where they're at. It's giving them exactly what they need with the kids they have in their classroom right now. Not some hypothetical class, not next year's group. The kids sitting in front of them today.

This is tailored support and coaching. It's professional development that actually develops the educator and expands their toolbox. It's messy and real and specific to your school, your challenges, your victories. And that's exactly what makes it work. It's intentional. And others notice the difference.

— CHAPTER 11 —

Redefining SUPPORT

Here's the most exciting part about redefining support: You get to choose who gives it to you. You get to decide who's in your herd. Your people don't have to be in the same building, same district, or even the same state. Honestly, some of the most soul-filling relationships I've ever had started with a comment on a post or a DM on Instagram. Because when you find someone who just gets it, someone who speaks your love language as an educator, it can feel like you've known them forever. That's exactly what happened when I met Jaime.

Jaime and I had only connected online, but the moment we started chatting, it was like she had cracked open my brain. She was my herd. She saw me. And when she invited me to Idaho to stay at her house, meet her husband and kids, and dream out loud together, I said yes. Well, I probably said, "Hell yes!" But you get it.

Some people might call that unwise, but I call it community. I flew out and stayed with her and her family, and it felt like we'd known each other for years. It was in her living room, on the floor of her office, around her kitchen table, and in her car driving to Redfish Lake with her pup that I truly learned the power of intentional connection.

Jaime didn't just give me a guest room and a warm welcome; she introduced me to even more of my people. That weekend, I met Dr.

Jayme. We sat for three hours over brunch, eating, chatting, and laughing our butts off. Three hours, y'all. And we talked about dreaming bigger, reaching more districts, and creating change in schools and homes across the nation. We didn't talk about test scores or lesson plans—we talked about vision, impact, and how to run into the storm together.

That meeting planted seeds that are still blooming today. It reminded me that your people don't have to be the ones you see every day. Your herd can be a Voxer thread, a podcast you listen to religiously, a social media group, or a community you haven't even fully stepped into yet. You just have to be open to finding them and be bold enough to say yes when they show up.

The truth is that the most powerful support isn't handed to you; it's built. It's born from shared values, from being seen, and from the courage to say, "You feel it too?" Finding your people means intentionally creating spaces where affirmation flows freely, where big dreams aren't scary, and where growth is celebrated, not judged.

We talk a lot about mentorship in education, but let's be real: Educators need more than just advice. We need affirmation, not exhaustion. Teachers need a community that supports them consistently and meaningfully. A community that doesn't just throw resources at them but surrounds them with love, understanding, and the kind of feedback that helps them grow. It's about creating a herd that holds you up, not one that makes you feel like you're drowning.

BE INTENTIONAL BY
redefining support
SO OTHERS NOTICE AFFIRMATION, NOT EXHAUSTION.

We need support. We need practice. And above all, we need people who understand that the work we do, day in and day out, isn't easy. We need to be intentional, not only with our students but with ourselves.

Real support isn't about handing off some curriculum or hosting a one-time PD session. It's about ongoing mentorship that you can adopt in your daily life, something that works for you. Imagine a world where teachers are consistently supported, where mentorship is part of the fabric of a school's culture. That's the kind of support I'm talking about, and it's not just a fleeting moment. It's about creating a system that builds on itself and brings people together in a way that matters.

Too many times, I've heard stories from educators who feel like they're not actually supported by the people who claim to be their biggest advocates. Being a mentor isn't just a title. It's about showing up. It's about becoming someone your colleagues feel safe with, someone they can trust for nonjudgmental feedback. We all need mentors who will stand up for us, not tear us down. It's through consistent love and support that teachers can truly transform.

Jenn, a teacher in New Jersey, has been working with me every week over Zoom for the past three years. We've built a strong relationship: No matter where she is in her teaching journey, I am always there to support her. It's been incredibly rewarding to see her grow, not only as an educator but as a person who has truly embraced social-emotional learning and the power of building strong, meaningful relationships with her students. Because yes, she is committed to this work for *them*. But she's also all in for herself.

When Jenn thinks of me, she says it feels like I'm right there with her during her school day, especially when challenges come up. We laugh about that idea. Like there's this little internal battle between the angel and the devil happening, and she needs to decide what she's going to do. I'm the angel on her shoulder, telling her to take a step back, pause, and not snap at the students. "You shouldn't have used that tone." "What are you thinking? You know better than that." And then there's that dang little devil telling her to slip back into her old ways. "Just tell them to put their heads down. Have them do it all over again." It's not about judgment. This is about support. I'm always there to remind her that her emotions are valid, but she has the tools to navigate those tricky moments and create a calm and empowering environment for her students.

One of the highlights of our coaching journey together has been the time I get to spend with Jenn inside her classroom. Once or twice a year, I fly out to New Jersey to work with her in person for an entire day. Or, if we're lucky, two full days. These in-person coaching sessions allow me to work directly alongside Jenn, coaching her in the moment. I can see firsthand how she interacts with her students, and we dive deep into the strategies and systems that help her maintain a calm presence while also fostering an environment of support and empowerment.

Jenn's students feel the difference. They're not just taught; they're seen and heard. They know she cares about them. And, as Jenn has learned, her ability to remain calm and approach each situation with empathy is a direct result of all the SEL that we've worked on together. We take time after each day in the classroom to reflect. No judgment, just a safe space for Jenn to process, learn, and grow. And it's usually over a glass of wine or two at her house, sitting by the fireplace or at her kitchen island. This makes that reflection time even better.

It's not just the social-emotional systems that run her classroom and support her students. It's that common language too. What we're really teaching kids is the hard stuff. We're teaching them how to persevere, how to tap into their emotional intelligence. Even third graders, like those in Jenn's classroom, need emotional regulation, peer relationships, growth mindset, all of it. And while it's not ever going to be perfect, and kids are still going to be kids, it's the learning and growth that matters.

No teacher evaluation or observation rubric could possibly measure the love and magic Jenn brings into that room every single day. Her kids come running into that classroom. They hug her, and they feel safe, calm, valued, and supported. Her BISON brag tag ceremonies will leave you absolutely speechless. Even the mindful moments are just so incredibly special. And those are the things that make her not just an effective educator but an exceptional one.

You know who else notices what Jenn is doing? Parents. The families in the community. Year after year, parents write emails to the principal begging for Jenn to teach their younger child, having done such an outstanding job with their elder one. They want their family to experience that magic again. And Jenn teaches the same strategies and brings the same language to family engagement nights. Instead of fluff, she holds meaningful sessions where she teaches parents how to bring all this into their homes. That's lasting impact. It's not just a morning meeting. This is social-emotional learning all day long, and it just feels different.

None of this happens by accident. The reason why her students, their families, and the community notice is because Jenn has been intentional. She invested in herself. She made the decision to surround herself with a mentor and a like-minded herd of educators across the nation who support each other and hold each other accountable. She's intentional about reminding herself to implement these systems in her classroom. She's intentional about creating a culture where students feel safe and empowered and where SEL is woven into every interaction. This level of intentionality is why Jenn's classroom is the kind of place that leaves such a lasting impact on everyone who walks through the door. And while Jenn's school may have another mascot, the BISON is always at the heart of her classroom. She lives the BISON mentality every day, being intentional in every action she takes, ensuring her students not only succeed but thrive in an environment where they feel heard, seen, and loved.

We need more relationships like this. We need more people who understand this deep, transformative work. Putting this into practice is hard. And shifting your mindset takes effort. But this is what really creates change in classrooms, in educators, in leaders, in communities, and in kids. And we need more people who are willing to flip that switch.

BECOME THE BISON

PRIORITIZE AUTHENTIC CONNECTION

This need for connection isn't just an adult thing—it starts early. Kids naturally gravitate toward their own herd. You've probably seen kids form social groups and thought, "Of course that kid started hanging out with so-and-so. They're exactly the same sort of people." Maybe it's their shared energy, common interests, or just a desire to belong.

In middle and high school especially, finding that group, the one that gets you, laughs with you, and lifts you, is everything. It's no different for us as adults. Whether you're navigating a classroom or raising a child, you need people who remind you that you're not doing it alone. Parenthood in particular demands a village. Sometimes your herd is the other mom at pickup who just gets it, and sometimes it's a Facebook group where you can ask questions without judgment, or a podcast that feels like a warm hug on a hard day. Finding your people, those who run at your pace, share your values, and show up for you, isn't a luxury. It's essential. Because when we run with the right herd, we're stronger, braver, and better equipped to face whatever comes our way.

In the hustle of daily demands, it's easy to fall into surface-level interactions, but becoming the BISON begins with intentional, values-based connection. When you prioritize authentic connection, you seek out people who energize you. It's those people who believe in the same mission and bring the same fire to the work. Maybe that looks like jumping on Voxer with a colleague after school to exchange ideas in real time, or perhaps it's joining a Marco Polo thread where you can share reflections throughout the week. These aren't just tools; they're lifelines when they're used with the right people.

But here's the tricky part. If someone in that space doesn't value authentic connection, they won't just fail to contribute—they'll drain the momentum. One bad apple in the group, one consistently negative voice, can erode trust and stifle collaboration, decreasing everyone's motivation and productivity. Trust me, I've facilitated too many groups on Voxer where a coach, district leader, teacher, or parent sucked the life right out of everyone. Because when they don't value this type of reflection and connection, it infects the group's overall energy.

On the flip side, when you're surrounded by a group of like-minded educators who are just as intentional as you about growing, reflecting, and supporting one another, it's rocket fuel. These are your people. They're the ones who text after a hard day, cheer you on in staff meetings, and push you to grow with love and truth. Connection with the right herd lifts you. It reminds you that you're not alone. Your energy becomes contagious. When you're aligned with others who match your values and pace, you don't just survive the hard stuff—you face it head-on, stronger, bolder, and more inspired. That's the power of a BISON herd.

SEEK AND OFFER MENTORSHIP

Mentorship is more than advice. It's a shared experience that builds connection, confidence, and community. When we intentionally seek out mentors, we allow ourselves to grow in ways we could never achieve alone. But the real magic happens when we offer our own wisdom and energy back.

A perfect example is a young teacher I coached in a district-wide cohort. She showed up to every Zoom session, contributed in our Voxer group, and stayed curious and open. She immersed herself in the community of learners around her. And because of that, she's now not only thriving in her own classroom but inviting others in. She's observing, being observed, and joining important conversations with her principal and peers. She's no longer just being mentored; she *is* a mentor. That's the cycle we need in education. One where growth is reciprocal and teachers feel supported enough to support others. They're not forced to mentor, not roped in or convinced that they need to in order to advance their career. But they naturally start mentoring others because the others have noticed the difference in that teacher.

Too often, mentorship in schools feels top-down, impersonal, or even performative. Teachers are usually plucked out and put into these positions. And it's not because they're exceptional mentors; it's just because the leaders know their teachers need support and some want to get out of their classrooms. Is this really the best way to provide mentorship? Is this what's best for teachers *or* kids? Teachers are paid a full-time teacher's salary to learn how to coach, produce slide decks, stand up and deliver content and PD, talk *at* teachers, and roll out the new curriculum and initiative in classrooms? We need to do better. We must do better. Coaching and mentorship needs to come from coaches and mentors. Ones who understand that classrooms thrive on social-emotional learning and who have experience from their own classrooms.

Because otherwise, educators are left feeling like another item on someone's checklist. They don't feel seen for the unique strengths they bring. That's why creating a culture of true mentorship—rooted in trust, reflection, and shared values—is vital. It can't be a one-off PD or a coaching title without a relationship. Real mentorship happens in the quiet moments of reflection, in the safe spaces where feedback feels like love, not judgment. It happens when someone like Jenn can hear my voice in her head—not as pressure but as a nudge toward intentionality. It's when teachers know they have people in their corner who help them show up fully without pretending everything's fine when it's not.

Mentorship is a two-way street. When we lean into both directions, we build something unstoppable. There is deep power in knowing that you're surrounded by people who push you to think bigger, reflect deeper, and lead stronger. And there's equal power in being that person for someone else. Whether you're brand new or a seasoned vet, you have something to offer and something to gain. This is how we create our BISON herd. We're not just running into challenges together. We're also lifting one another as we go. When educators are mentored with intention and then offer that same intentionality to others, they don't just grow; they transform. And they bring everyone around them along for the ride.

SET BOUNDARIES WITH INTENTION

Setting boundaries with intention isn't about shutting people out. It's about tuning into what feels aligned and honoring what fuels your purpose. When I said yes to my friend Jaime in Idaho, it wasn't about ignoring boundaries; it was about feeling a deep yes in my gut. There was clarity in our shared expectations. We were going to work on a project together, collaborate, create. And that's the thing about boundaries: They don't always come with rigid rules. Sometimes they show up in the form of intuitive alignment. Does this feel like a meaningful use of my time, my energy, my heart? Then yes. If not, if something feels off, forced, or draining, that's your signal to pause, redirect, or say not *yet* or not at all. Intention is the compass, not an obligation.

So many of us were raised as yes people. We take on more, do more, make ourselves available and agreeable. But when we say yes to everything, we often end up saying no to ourselves. Saying no doesn't have to be harsh. It can sound like "Now's not the best time," "Let me think on that," or "This isn't the right fit for me right now." When we set boundaries with kindness and clarity, we're not just protecting our peace; we're modeling it for others. We're showing our students, our colleagues, and our families that it's okay to choose what feels right, and we don't have to explain ourselves endlessly to do it.

Trust me, I'm still working on this. Sometimes—most of the time, actually—I find myself feeling frustrated by the people around me. Why won't that district leader take care of that email right now? Why won't my son put away his clean laundry as soon as it's ready for him? Why won't that principal get their coaching days scheduled? Why doesn't my spouse see that we need to change the filter and just automatically do it? Why do they need a hundred reminders before they take action?

It's important for all of us, me and my brain especially, to remember that we are not in control of the people around us. We're not in control of the things they feel need to be done or the order in which they do those things. Hell, we're not even in control of whether they like us, want to be around us, or allow us to be part of that fantasy football league anymore.

But when we're intentional with our time and energy, we become more effective as educators, parents, partners, and leaders. We show up with more presence and less resentment. We stop running on fumes and start operating from fullness because there's more gas in our tanks. We create space for both purpose and pause, and this allows us to lead, and live, with clarity and joy. Boundaries remind us that we can't do it all, but we can do what matters most.

PRACTICE SPECIFIC APPRECIATION

When we're all trying our best, which we usually are, it matters deeply to be seen. Not in a vague or passing way but in a way that tells us someone noticed exactly how we showed up. Specific appreciation is one of the most powerful tools we have to boost morale, strengthen relationships, and build a culture of trust and belonging. It's not just "Thank you for your hard work." It's "Thank you for the way you handled that tough parent conversation with such clarity and compassion." That kind of intentional recognition is fuel. It confirms that our strengths aren't just present; they're impactful. And when parents receive that same kind of specific appreciation from teachers ("I see how much time you've spent helping your child with reading at home, and it's making such a difference"), they feel seen, valued, and invited into the team. That kind of connection is everything.

Telling the people in your herd how specific things make you feel is such a gift. I can't tell you how many times I hear this from my mentor teachers: "Wow, no one's told me that before." And the things I've said to them are so simple: "I loved the tone of your voice when you were talking to that teacher," or "I watched you get down low when you were coaching and it was absolute perfection," or "The intention that you set today with our group was pure gold," or "I'm thinking that you should totally do that Zoom session on your own tonight. You've got this."

These things push my mentor teachers out of their comfort zones and pull them into the unknown. But it also validates that what they're doing is on the right track, they're seen and valued, and they're worthy of more.

Being specific in your appreciation is contagious. When you model it, gratitude spills over among the people around you. Others begin to look for the good too. I hear my mentor teachers coaching the teachers in our community and the school districts that we work with. And they're pouring into them in the same way. It causes a ripple effect among educators all across the nation. Because you know what happens then? Our teachers do the same thing for their students. And those students grow into the next generation of adults who know *how* to practice gratitude and to intentionally show appreciation toward the people around them.

Teaching often feels thankless, parenting can feel isolating, and this small shift can be everything. It's how we build environments where people don't just survive the work—they feel proud of it. Because when we name each other's gifts, we remind one another that we matter. Not just for what we do but for how we do it. That's what holds a community together.

ADVOCATE FOR MEANINGFUL SUPPORT

Intentionally voice your needs and advocate for the resources, development opportunities, and recognition that will truly make a difference for you and your colleagues.

Because let's be honest: Too many teachers are silently struggling. We're told to "take care of ourselves" while being handed another initiative, another module, another meeting that leaves us feeling more isolated than before. What we actually need isn't more content; it's connection.

Real support doesn't come from a slide deck. It comes from someone who notices when we're running on empty and offers to walk beside us, not ahead of us. Advocating for meaningful support means giving ourselves permission to say, "This isn't working," then asking boldly for what will. That might be time. It might be mentorship. It might be someone to sit with you after school and simply listen.

Sometimes advocating means refusing to let bureaucracy break what's working. When my mentee Taylor had to transfer schools after her first year due to declining enrollment, we both faced a heartbreaking reality. The induction program's rules dictated that mentors should be at the same school site because it had just always been done that way. We were told it would be better for her support system, but sitting there together, both of us in tears at the thought of losing our connection, *we* knew better. This wasn't just about following protocol; it was about preserving a relationship that had become essential to both of us.

In that moment, we made a choice that surprised even us: We decided to advocate. Not just for Taylor's need to keep me as her mentor but for my need to keep mentoring her. Because real mentorship isn't about proximity or convenience. It's about the trust and understanding that grows between two people committed to each other's growth. We challenged the system not out of defiance but out of love for what we had built together. And in doing so, we discovered that sometimes the most powerful advocacy happens when we refuse to accept "that's just how it's always been done" as an answer.

When we start speaking up—not in complaint, but in courage—we open the door for others to do the same. It's not about demanding more for the sake of it. It's about redefining what support actually looks like. Sometimes, it looks like coaching that doesn't feel evaluative. Sometimes, it's leadership that asks how you really are. And sometimes, it's just someone telling you, "You're doing better than you think." We can't keep pretending the system works when so many of us feel unseen inside of it.

And don't forget the power of celebration. Advocating for support also means creating space to celebrate our kids—and one another. Those celebrations aren't just for scores or outcomes but for showing up, for growing, for being human. It's easy to overlook those moments when you're constantly spinning in survival mode, but they're the moments that bring us back to life. So let's advocate, not just for ourselves but for a culture where support is human, connection is intentional, and celebration is part of the work. That's how we build something that lasts. That's how we run stronger, together.

— CHAPTER 12 —

Connecting with FAMILIES

Education has been fragmented for too long. Administrators meet separately. Teachers attend workshops alone. Specialists work in isolation. Parents hold their own meetings. What if we could bring all these voices together to work toward the same goal?

When I think about the struggles of neurodivergent kids in school, my heart aches. I'm part of my mama community whose children navigate these challenges. One thread that runs through our conversations is the frustration we feel when teachers faced with big behaviors are simply told to write kids up. When a child elopes, shows aggression, or struggles with self-regulation, the response from many schools is a write-up, a consequence, a punishment. But what is this really doing to the child?

These kids are doing the best they can with the skills they have. They're not misbehaving out of defiance. They're struggling because they don't yet have the tools to respond differently. Punishing a child for lagging skills isn't just ineffective; it's damaging. Instead of teaching kids how to regulate their emotions, we're pushing them further away from success.

We need a complete transformation. We need systems rooted in understanding, empathy, and teaching. We need to move beyond writing kids up every time they fall short and start teaching the skills they lack. When we provide the right interventions and help students develop emotional regulation and coping strategies, we create environments where they can thrive.

This is why we have to break down the silos between home and school, between teachers and parents, between specialists and administrators. We need a unified front that addresses not just the behaviors but the underlying skills that need development. The foundation of this transformation starts with one critical change:

BE INTENTIONAL BY *connecting with* FAMILIES SO OTHERS NOTICE COMMUNITY, NOT ISOLATION.

When we actively reach out to parents as partners rather than adversaries, when we create spaces for genuine collaboration rather than compliance meetings, we begin to model what unified support looks like. Educators, administrators, and students themselves start to see what's possible when we choose connection over separation. This approach transforms school culture from the inside out.

BECOME THE BISON

BREAK THE SILOS

That's where real change begins. For too long, educators, administrators, parents, and even students have been operating in isolation, each carrying the weight of the system without fully seeing or hearing one another. One of my favorite things, especially as a woman in business, has always been gathering people together. It lights something up in me. And over the years, I've come to realize that our education system won't shift until we start bringing all the voices to the same table. Not just educators across the nation but the district leaders making the calls—and perhaps most importantly, the parents and students. They are the ones who are most affected.

That's why I have Lucie speak at all my events. That's why I have her mother speak. That's why I have teachers speak. That's why I have specialists speak. As a student who struggles with all things social and emotional, Lucie offers a perspective that cuts through the noise. And when parents and educators get the chance to ask her questions directly, to see what it's like through her eyes, something powerful happens. Walls come down. Understanding deepens. That's what we get when we stop talking about each other and start talking with each other.

But it can't just happen once a year. Real collaboration isn't a conference—it's a continuous commitment. Yes, we need those big, energizing spaces where the whole community can come together. But we also need the smaller, more intimate circles where real relationships are built, where voices don't get lost in the crowd. Because this work, the real work, isn't about theory. It's about action. Too often, we sit in rooms filled with fluff, talking in circles about what should change instead of mapping out how to actually make it happen. Becoming the BISON means we don't just talk. We move. Together. And when we do, we make sure everyone walks away with their own next best steps, whether they're at the front of a classroom, leading a district, or raising a child at home.

Educators are exhausted. Many are working in silos, barely able to connect with colleagues outside of their hallway, let alone their district. Yet their needs, ideas, and innovations are often exactly what a parent or administrator in another city is desperate to hear. Our eyes need to be wide open. The only way to create sustainable transformation in education is to zoom out past our school walls, past our zip codes, and into a shared vision. When we unite our voices, we don't just create awareness; we create momentum. And momentum leads to action. That's how we move from isolation to impact.

USE EMOTIONS AS DATA

When we're building intentional connections with families, one of the most powerful shifts we can make is to start seeing behaviors as communication rather than disruption. Every child who yells, shuts down, hits, hides, or storms out is trying to tell us something important. And when we listen deeply, not just to students but to their families, we begin to notice the stories behind those behaviors.

Think about the parent who constantly receives phone calls about their child's behavior. They hear the frustration in the teacher's voice, the list of what went wrong, the consequences that follow. Over time, that parent begins to wonder if their child is fundamentally flawed. But what if we approached that same conversation differently? What if we started with curiosity instead of judgment?

The shift happens when we see behaviors as data. That data is telling us where a child is struggling and where we, as the adults, have the opportunity to support and teach.

This means moving beyond surface-level compliance to understand the lagging skills underneath. The child who can't sit still might be telling us about sensory needs. The student who explodes when plans change is showing us they need support with cognitive flexibility. The kid who shuts down during group work might be communicating that they need help with perspective-taking or social problem-solving.

When we bring this lens to our conversations with families, everything changes. Instead of asking parents what consequences work at home, we might ask them what they've noticed makes their child feel calm. Instead of listing problems, we start exploring patterns together.

We become partners in understanding this child's unique needs rather than adversaries trying to fix their behavior.

This approach recognizes that our discipline systems often rely on compliance instead of connection. When we default to "fixing" a behavior rather than understanding its root, we reinforce shame instead of building skills. But when we use emotions as data, we create space for healing and growth. And that growth is experienced by the child, the family, and the school community.

The truth is that we cannot expect what we haven't taught. We need to teach social and emotional skills, not expect them. If we want children to be safe, kind, and responsible, we need to explicitly teach the skills that make those behaviors possible. And we need to do this work in partnership with families, honoring their insights about their child while sharing our observations from the school setting.

When we approach challenging behaviors with curiosity and empathy, we unlock something powerful. We see the opportunity to build skills instead of break spirits, to create connection instead of isolation, and to support the whole child in becoming who they're meant to be. And we become stronger, more compassionate humans (or BISON) because of it.

TEACH INTO LAGGING SKILLS

A mom in my community once opened up an email from her child's teacher. It was the kind of email that stings before you even finish reading. It said things like "disrespectful," "won't follow directions," and "refuses to participate." But what broke this mom was the way no one seemed to see what she saw—a child who wanted to do the right thing but didn't yet have the skills.

She said to me, "He's not trying to be disrespectful. He just doesn't know how to do what they're asking." In that moment, she felt like the school had stopped seeing her son as a whole person and started seeing him as a problem to solve. That's when it hit me. How often are we punishing kids for their missing skills instead of teaching them? Why are we isolating families instead of inviting them into a partnership?

We expect regulation from dysregulation. Flexibility from rigidity. Social understanding from confusion. But these are skills, and just like reading or math, they have to be taught, again and again, with consistency, compassion, and clarity shared between home and school.

At home, this might look like taping a visual schedule near the bathroom mirror or creating a picture list of what "getting ready for school" means. But here's what makes this powerful: When schools and families use the same language, the same visual supports, the same previewing strategies, children feel consistency instead of confusion. You might sit down every evening to preview the next day so your child feels safe and calm. When that preview includes what their teacher will be working on with them, families become partners in the learning, not just recipients of behavior reports.

In the classroom, it's not just about having a calm corner or feelings chart, though those help. It's about intentionally front-loading before the hard moments come and then sharing those strategies with families so the support doesn't stop at the school door. Before independent work, group time, or recess, talk about what tools they can use, what success looks like, and what to do if things get hard. Then send that same road map home. That's what true partnership looks like. Not waiting until the explosion but anticipating the spark, then handing both the child and their family strategies instead of taking it personally.

Because if we aren't building systems that teach kids how to solve problems, regulate emotions, and make progress, systems that bridge home and school, we're just reacting in isolation, and that cycle doesn't break itself.

And for our leaders, your role is crucial in creating connection, not division. What kind of culture are you creating? One where teachers feel supported in teaching missing skills alongside families or one where they're told to "write it up" so you can collect data and move on? Supporting a student means supporting the team around that student, and that team includes their family. It means real conversations where we share not just what's challenging but what we're actively teaching and how families can support it at home. It means clarity on what's missing and a plan that goes deeper than seating charts and behavior logs. It's a plan that invites families and the children into the solution.

Are we offering tools that match real needs and can be used consistently across settings, or are we just reshuffling the same old consequences that leave families feeling blamed and isolated? Because thriving classrooms don't grow from punishment or from keeping families at arm's length. They grow from purpose. They grow when we stop asking how to make kids behave and start asking what they need to succeed and how can we build that *together*. That's the difference. That's the shift from isolation to community. That's becoming the BISON.

BUILD BRAVE SPACES FOR CHANGE

There's nothing that drains my spirit faster than walking into a professional development session where the tables are draped in white linens, the water glasses are sweating, the air conditioning is blasting like we're in a meat locker, and everyone takes out their laptops and stares at their screens.

You sit quietly, probably toward the back, maybe with people you don't know. There's a forced hush in the room, and then—cue the speaker. They take the podium and begin flipping through a fifty-slide deck, reading every single word aloud. You glance around. No one's moved. No one's engaged. No one's changed. Everyone's on their laptop, or worse, their cell phone.

These sessions aren't brave. They're stale. They're packed with theory, buried in jargon, and void of action. It's no wonder people walk out of these rooms uninspired, overwhelmed, unchanged. That's not what this work is about. That's not what *we* are about.

Real change starts when people feel seen, heard, and safe to be vulnerable. Think about what we do when we come home. I kick off my shoes, take a deep breath, wrap myself in a blanket, or crack open a cold drink. The type of day I've had affects the type of cold drink I'm holding.

That's when my nervous system starts to settle. That's when we're most open to growth. That's how professional development should feel. We need to create brave spaces, safe ones, where educators, parents, and leaders can show up as they are, share stories, and speak truth without fear of being dismissed or judged.

The goal isn't perfection; it's connection and momentum. It's being surrounded by people who "get it," who nod along when you say, "This part is really hard." These are the people who ask, "How can we move forward—together?" Because that's what ignites change. We need clear, personalized action steps that meet people where they are and help them take one intentional step forward, knowing they're not walking alone.

No one needs another slide deck. They need belonging. They need practical tools that work across home and school. They need to walk away not just with a handout but with hope and next steps that feel doable in the chaos of real life. That means we stop leading from slides and start leading from stories. We ask what's actually happening in classrooms, homes, and hearts. We center the voices that are usually left out, especially the families. They know their children best. And we design experiences that don't just fill time but fuel transformation and build bridges between all the adults who care about the kids.

That's how we build brave spaces for change: by trading in podiums for connection, theory for action, and white tablecloths for warmth. Let's stop trying to impress and start trying to impact. That's where the revolution lives. That's why I created ViBE EDU. An "unconference" that creates this type of experience and brings together all voices, even the voices of our students. A space where we come with intention and leave with action. And trust me, it's quite the vibe.

Picture this: an open space where conversations matter more than presentations. Where you can float between sessions, hear what people are actually doing in their classrooms, and ask questions that get real answers and action steps. Where we wipe away the old notion of the "sage on the stage" and instead bring everybody together—as equals, as partners—in driving the change we desperately want to see in our students, our schools, and ourselves.

It's dynamic. It's alive. There are no slide decks, no podiums, no silos. Just a space where every voice has a seat at the table because we built this table together. You feel the energy, the collaboration, and the intention in every detail. If you want to be part of a transformation that actually sticks, you need to experience it. Teaching Inside Out's first ViBE EDU conference in Anaheim, California, was just the beginning—a taste of what's possible when curiosity, courage, and connection lead the way.

LEAD WITH THE BISON MENTALITY

The only constant in education, and in life, is change. Our students' brains are rewiring themselves daily, responding to a world that evolves faster than we can track. Technology shifts. Expectations rise. And our children will grow into futures we can't yet imagine. We can't hold on to old systems and expect them to work for new generations. And we can't expect ourselves to shoulder the weight of this transformation alone. Change is not a solo sport. It's a collective charge, and the ones who lead it must do so together, hand in hand with the families and communities they serve.

But let's be honest: Who you run with matters. One toxic teammate or one chronically negative voice can drain your energy, derail your progress, and dim your fire. The herd you choose is everything. Because the right people don't just stand beside you; they remind you who you are when you forget. They push you forward when you're stuck. They say, "Let's go" when the storm rolls in. And they believe in building bridges, not walls.

Whether you're tuning into our *Unleashing the BISON* podcast, joining the Becoming the BISON Facebook community, investing in yourself through our SELebrate Good Times retreats, attending the ViBE EDU conference, or partnering with Teaching Inside Out to reimagine your school or district, you are surrounding yourself with a herd that fuels growth, not fear. Hope, not burnout. Momentum, not stagnation. Connection, not isolation.

So this is your moment. You've read the words and you've felt the fire. And if I've written these words the way I intended, the path forward is clear. Connecting with families isn't just strategy; it's the heart of transformation.

When we choose community over isolation, build bridges instead of walls, we become the change our kids need. Leading with the BISON mentality includes every voice. Every family—every person who cares about kids—gets to run into the storm together, united. That's the heartbeat of this movement. That's what it means to become the BISON. And that's how we create the revolution our kids and our hearts have been waiting for.

The question isn't whether you're ready for this revolution. The question is this: Are you ready to become who you need to be to transform *through* this?

PART IV

THE BISON *Revolution*

— CHAPTER 13 —

It's About **YOU**

As I write this, it's only been a few days since I got home from visiting more schools to support more teachers and students. I only have a few days before I fly back out and do it all over again. Let me tell you, I am exhausted.

But this is the work I was born to do. And I know this because when I'm there, in the moment, speaking with teachers, guiding them in their work, supporting them in their classrooms, modeling just how incredible their classrooms can feel, I'm living my dream.

And this work includes the book you're reading. It's not just about social-emotional learning, or behaviors, or curriculum, or standards. It's about being a teacher for the teachers. It's about getting into your brains, your classrooms, the behaviors and expectations that you have for your students, then showing you, guiding you, supporting you. Are you ready for what comes after that? Here it is: It's about empowering you to do the work on your own.

And guess what? It's already happening. When I sat down this morning to plan my next few Instagram posts—you know, what entrepreneurs do in their "spare time"—I was going to search for videos of me working in the over twenty-five classrooms I was in last week. I was about to reach out to one of the teachers and ask her for some footage when suddenly it dawned on me: This post wasn't about me. It was about them. It was about the amazing work that they were doing. It was about the phenomenal team of ambassadors they created. My herd. Our herd. They're out there grabbing these new strategies and systems by the horns and diving headfirst into the work.

We've talked about that work throughout this book. The intentional connections with families that break through isolation. The understanding that behaviors are data, not disruptions. The recognition that we cannot expect what we haven't taught. The commitment to building skills instead of breaking spirits. These educators aren't just implementing strategies; they're transforming their entire approach to teaching and learning.

THE BISON WITHIN YOU

We are always going to have students with tricky behaviors. We're always going to look out at our classroom and see outliers. We're going to go deep into our bag of tricks and start pulling out all the stops. And we're also going to get to a point where we just can't do it anymore. Our bag of tricks is almost empty. We don't have the language, we don't have the phrases, we don't have the strategies, tools, or systems to support our students and their needs. We're going to become frustrated. We're going to feel worn out and overwhelmed.

And guess what? More and more things are going to be added to your plate. There will be more changes to the curriculum. The grading system will change over and over again. That pendulum will continue to swing. But you get to choose what you do about it. Will you follow others even though you know it's the wrong fit? Or will you become the BISON?

The educators who just go along will end up bitter and exhausted. They will walk through the halls of your schools and whisper. They'll complain to each other, to your administration, and to anyone else who will listen to them. They'll make threats. Threats to go to the district office, threats to send students out of the classroom, and threats to leave the profession altogether. They'll meet up with their like-minded colleagues and continue the cycle of toxic negativity in the lunchroom. They'll march through the halls with their heads held high, as if they're standing their ground, but you know what happens? The walls in those schools become heavy. You walk through those classrooms and you can feel the difference. There's an absence. An absence of heart, soul, passion, fire, and genuine love. That love that drove you to teach. That empathetic vision you had when you first came into this profession. It's gone.

But it doesn't have to be this way. You can feel supported, loved, and guided. Because, my dear educators, you deserve to feel like this. You deserve to feel every single ounce of love and true support. You don't need to feel overwhelmed, frustrated, and drained. You need a lifeboat, not a kickboard, as you go through your days. You need a community that will give you the support you actually need, not the support they think you need. Your days can feel easier. You truly can thrive. But here's the secret: It starts with you.

You must find the BISON within you. Find who you get to become. Choose to head into that storm. Even when it's ugly. Even when you're frustrated and scared. Even when others are trying to convince you to run away. Even when fear gets in your head and tells you it's time to tap out. It won't be easy. Know that. But guess what? It will be oh so worth it.

You see, it's my mission to continue to grow my herd of BISON. My community is filled with educators who are being intentional. They know that there are big behaviors, they realize that curriculum is being changed or added to their already overflowing plate, they've seen students come into their classrooms and thought, "I don't know how to help this kid." But instead of running away, instead of arguing or talking negatively about their admin, district, other teachers, families, or kids, they ran into that storm and did something about it.

They understand that every challenging behavior is communication. They've learned to see emotions as data. They've built authentic partnerships with families instead of adversarial relationships. They've created classrooms where students feel safe to be vulnerable, where mistakes are learning opportunities, where connection comes before correction. They've embraced the truth that we cannot expect what we haven't taught, and they've committed to teaching the skills that matter most.

They know that they can't do it alone. They know that they need to feel supported. And they know everything will be easier because they have a herd of like-minded BISON to connect and collaborate with. No competition, no negativity. Just community and intentional action that other people start to notice. And that, my friends, is what the BISON mentality is all about.

When you choose to be the BISON, you're not just changing your own experience. You're changing the experience of every student who walks into your classroom. You're changing the dynamic with every family you partner with. You're shifting the culture of your school, your district, your entire educational community. You're proving that there's another way to do this work, a way that honors both the complexity of human behavior and the incredible potential that exists within every child.

So what are you waiting for? The future of education is in your hands. The power to transform your teaching, your school, your district, your life, and the lives of your students and their families lies within you. Choose yourself. Invest in yourself. Join the BISON revolution. Your herd is waiting for you.

This is the year you focus on who, not how.

This is the year you find your people.

This is the year you fear less.

This is the year you remember consistency over intensity.

This is the year you make decisions with intention.

This is the year you take action.

This is the year you run with your herd.
This is the year you focus on yourself.
This is the year you run into the storms.
This is the year you become the BISON.
Be intentional so others notice.
I can't wait to notice the difference in you.
The work is hard. The work is worthy. The work is you.
Welcome to the herd.

Acknowledgments

To my teacher community, my herd.

You are the heartbeat of this work and the reason *Becoming the BISON* exists. Every message you sent, every story you shared, and every moment you trusted me with your classroom, your students, or your courage shaped these pages. You wake up each day and choose connection over convenience, intention over autopilot, and impact over overwhelm. Thank you for letting me run alongside you. Thank you for believing that change is possible and for proving it, one brave choice at a time. This book is as much yours as it is mine.

To the educators who welcomed me into your schools, your meetings, your classrooms, and your hearts, thank you for allowing me to witness your brilliance, your honesty, and your willingness to evolve. You have shown me that the BISON mentality is alive and thriving in teachers everywhere. My hope is that you see yourself in these pages, because so much of this work grew from your courage and your stories.

To my husband, thank you for your patience through late nights, early mornings, and the moments when my mind was tucked inside a chapter instead of the room we were in. Your encouragement and humor kept me grounded, and your belief made it possible to keep going. You are my safe place, my motivation, and my joy.

To my son, who teaches me each day what it means to be intentional, empathetic, and brave, you are woven into every chapter, every story, and every piece of this mission. This book carries pieces of you.

To the parents, students, administrators, and fellow humans who have entrusted me with your stories, thank you. You are the reason I remain committed to this work. You remind me that education is not a system, it is a community, a living and breathing herd.

And to every person who has ever felt alone in a classroom, overwhelmed by expectations, or unsure whether you were making a difference, this book was written with you in mind. May these pages give you the courage to run into the storm with intention and the confidence that you never have to run alone.

Thank you for being part of this journey. Thank you for being part of this herd, because no one does meaningful work alone.

About the AUTHOR

Kim Gameroz is an educational changemaker and SEL-focused coach who brings nearly twenty years of leadership, clarity, and compassion to schools across the country. As the founder of Teaching Inside Out®, she works with districts to build effective teaching frameworks and Tier I behavior supports that move campuses from reacting to leading with purpose.

She is also the creator of SELebrate Good Times®, a community of educators that reshapes how professional learning feels. Through coaching, live events, and the Bloom retreat, Kim creates environments where educators learn through connection, belonging, and genuine renewal.

Her work is rooted in the BISON mentality and her message, Be Intentional So Others Notice®. Kim encourages educators and students to meet challenges with clarity and courage, believing that we grow stronger when we stop carrying the work alone.

Kim lives in Dallas, Texas, with her husband, Shaun, and their son, Wyatt—her daily reminder of why intentionality matters.

Bring the **BISON MENTALITY** *to Your School*

Change takes root when people grow together. Programs alone cannot shift a culture. Connected, courageous, and intentional educators can. The BISON mentality creates the conditions for that kind of transformation—where adults feel empowered, relationships strengthen, and students experience emotional safety and belonging every single day. When schools embrace the BISON mentality, they step into a collective courage that's grounded in community, clarity, and action.

KEYNOTE SPEAKING: BECOMING THE BISON

Becoming the BISON is Kim's signature keynote and the heartbeat of this book—a keynote designed to elevate courage, strengthen connection, and inspire schoolwide transformation. At a time when traditional behavior approaches rely on control and compliance, leaving educators overwhelmed and students misunderstood, Becoming the BISON offers a different way forward. Through vivid storytelling and real classroom moments, Kim shows teams how to view behavior through the lens of emotional intelligence, executive functioning, and SEL, helping educators understand what students can do versus what they are still learning to manage.

Kim equips educators with the tools to Be Intentional So Others Notice® and the mindset to lead change with confidence. She helps teams see behavior as communication, relationships as the foundation of learning, and their own work through a lens of clarity and purpose. The keynote weaves together the principles of redesigning behavior, disability awareness, and proactive classroom design—giving educators both the "why" and the "how" to create environments where all students can thrive, especially those with invisible disabilities or executive functioning challenges.

Educators leave with the momentum to:

- Move from surviving to leading
- Rebuild connection in classrooms and teams
- Reduce overwhelm through clarity, systems, and intention
- Renew their sense of purpose during a time when it matters most
- Step into courage, change, and becoming

Administrators and district leaders often describe Kim's keynotes as the spark their staff needed to move forward together. Schools report renewed belief in what is possible, stronger teamwork, and a shared language that anchors their daily work. What begins as inspiration becomes a shift in mindset, and that shift becomes lasting cultural impact.

If you want professional development that ignites real transformation—a keynote that unites your staff, strengthens your systems, and builds a culture where every student is seen, supported, and valued—invite Kim to bring the BISON mentality to your school or district. The next step begins when you reach out.

TEACHINGINSIDEOUT.COM

More from

Dave Burgess Consulting, Inc.

Since 2012, DBCI has published books that inspire and equip educators to be their best. For more information on our titles or to purchase bulk orders for your school, district, or book study, visit DaveBurgessConsulting.com/DBCIbooks.

THE *LIKE A PIRATE™* SERIES

Teach Like a PIRATE by Dave Burgess

Balance Like a PIRATE by Jessica Cabeen, Jessica Johnson, and Sarah Johnson

eXPlore Like a PIRATE by Michael Matera

Learn Like a PIRATE by Paul Solarz

Plan Like a PIRATE by Dawn M. Harris

Play Like a PIRATE by Quinn Rollins

Run Like a PIRATE by Adam Welcome

Tech Like a PIRATE by Matt Miller

THE *LEAD LIKE A PIRATE™* SERIES

Lead Like a PIRATE by Shelley Burgess and Beth Houf

Lead Beyond Your Title by Nili Bartley

Lead with Appreciation by Amber Teamann and Melinda Miller

Lead with Collaboration by Allyson Apsey and Jessica Gomez

Lead with Culture by Jay Billy

Lead with Instructional Rounds by Vicki Wilson

Lead with Literacy by Mandy Ellis

She Leads by Dr. Rachael George and Majalise W. Tolan

THE EDUPROTOCOL FIELD GUIDE SERIES

Deploying EduProtocols by Kim Voge, with Jon Corippo and Marlena Hebern

The EduProtocol Field Guide by Marlena Hebern and Jon Corippo

The EduProtocol Field Guide Book 2 by Marlena Hebern and Jon Corippo

The EduProtocol Field Guide ELA Edition by Jacob Carr

The EduProtocol Field Guide Math Edition by Lisa Nowakowski and Jeremiah Ruesch

The EduProtocol Field Guide Primary Edition by Benjamin Cogswell and Jennifer Dean

The EduProtocol Field Guide Social Studies Edition by Dr. Scott M. Petri and Adam Moler

LEADERSHIP & SCHOOL CULTURE

Autopilot by Rich Czyz

Be 1% Better by Ron Clark

Be THAT Teacher by Dwayne Reed

Beyond the Surface of Restorative Practices by Marisol Rerucha

Change the Narrative by Henry J. Turner and Kathy Lopes

Choosing to See by Pamela Seda and Kyndall Brown

Culturize by Jimmy Casas

Discipline Win by Andy Jacks

Educate Me! by Dr. Shree Walker with Michael D. Ison

Escaping the School Leader's Dunk Tank by Rebecca Coda and Rick Jetter

Fight Song by Kim Bearden

From Teacher to Leader by Starr Sackstein

If the Dance Floor Is Empty, Change the Song by Joe Clark

The Innovator's Mindset by George Couros

It's OK to Say "They" by Christy Whittlesey

Kids Deserve It! by Todd Nesloney and Adam Welcome

Leading the Whole Teacher by Allyson Apsey

Let Them Speak by Rebecca Coda and Rick Jetter

The Limitless School by Abe Hege and Adam Dovico

Live Your Excellence by Jimmy Casas

Next-Level Teaching by Jonathan Alsheimer

The Pepper Effect by Sean Gaillard

Principaled by Kate Barker, Kourtney Ferrua, and Rachael George

The Principled Principal by Jeffrey Zoul and Anthony McConnell

Relentless by Hamish Brewer

The Secret Solution by Todd Whitaker, Sam Miller, and Ryan Donlan

Start. Right. Now. by Todd Whitaker, Jeffrey Zoul, and Jimmy Casas

Stop. Right. Now. by Jimmy Casas and Jeffrey Zoul

Teach Your Class Off by CJ Reynolds

Teachers Deserve It by Rae Hughart and Adam Welcome

They Call Me "Mr. De" by Frank DeAngelis

Thrive Through the Five by Jill M. Siler

Unmapped Potential by Julie Hasson and Missy Lennard

When Kids Lead by Todd Nesloney and Adam Dovico

Word Shift by Joy Kirr

Your School Rocks by Ryan McLane and Eric Lowe

TECHNOLOGY & TOOLS

50 Things to Go Further with Google Classroom by Alice Keeler and Libbi Miller

50 Things You Can Do with Google Classroom by Alice Keeler and Libbi Miller

50 Ways to Engage Students with Google Apps by Alice Keeler and Heather Lyon

140 Twitter Tips for Educators by Brad Currie, Billy Krakower, and Scott Rocco

AI Optimism by Becky Keene

Block Breaker by Brian Aspinall

Building Blocks for Tiny Techies by Jamila "Mia" Leonard

Code Breaker by Brian Aspinall

The Complete EdTech Coach by Katherine Goyette and Adam Juarez

Control Alt Achieve by Eric Curts

The Esports Education Playbook by Chris Aviles, Steve Isaacs, Christine Lion-Bailey, and Jesse Lubinsky

Google Apps for Littles by Christine Pinto and Alice Keeler

Master the Media by Julie Smith

Raising Digital Leaders by Jennifer Casa-Todd

Reality Bytes by Christine Lion-Bailey, Jesse Lubinsky, and Micah Shippee, PhD

Sail the 7 Cs with Microsoft Education by Becky Keene and Kathi Kersznowski

Shake Up Learning by Kasey Bell

Social LEADia by Jennifer Casa-Todd

Stepping Up to Google Classroom by Alice Keeler and Kimberly Mattina

Teaching Math with Google Apps by Alice Keeler and Diana Herrington

Teaching with Google Jamboard by Alice Keeler and Kimberly Mattina

Teachingland by Amanda Fox and Mary Ellen Weeks

TEACHING METHODS & MATERIALS

All 4s and 5s by Andrew Sharos

Boredom Busters by Katie Powell

Building Strong Writers by Christina Schneider

The Classroom Chef by John Stevens and Matt Vaudrey

The Collaborative Classroom by Trevor Muir

Copyrighteous by Diana Gill

CREATE by Bethany J. Petty

Ditch That Homework by Matt Miller and Alice Keeler

Ditch That Textbook by Matt Miller

Don't Ditch That Tech by Matt Miller, Nate Ridgway, and Angelia Ridgway

EDrenaline Rush by John Meehan

Educated by Design by Michael Cohen, The Tech Rabbi

Empowered to Choose: A Practical Guide to Personalized Learning by Andrew Easton

Expedition Science by Becky Schnekser

Frustration Busters by Katie Powell

Fully Engaged by Michael Matera and John Meehan

Game On? Brain On! by Lindsay Portnoy, PhD

Guided Math AMPED by Reagan Tunstall

Happy & Resilient by Roni Habib

Innovating Play by Jessica LaBar-Twomy and Christine Pinto

Instant Relevance by Denis Sheeran

Instructional Coaching Connection by Nathan Lang-Raad

Keeping the Wonder by Jenna Copper, Ashley Bible, Abby Gross, and Staci Lamb

LAUNCH by John Spencer and A.J. Juliani

Learning in the Zone by Dr. Sonny Magana

Less Talk, More Action by Allyson Apsey and Emily Freeland

Lights, Cameras, TEACH! by Kevin J. Butler

Make Learning MAGICAL by Tisha Richmond

Pass the Baton by Kathryn Finch and Theresa Hoover

Project-Based Learning Anywhere by Lori Elliott

Pure Genius by Don Wettrick

The Revolution by Darren Ellwein and Derek McCoy

The Science Box by Kim Adsit and Adam Peterson

Shift This! by Joy Kirr

Skyrocket Your Teacher Coaching by Michael Cary Sonbert

Spark Learning by Ramsey Musallam

Sparks in the Dark by Travis Crowder and Todd Nesloney

Table Talk Math by John Stevens

Teachables by Cheryl Abla and Lisa Maxfield

Unpack Your Impact by Naomi O'Brien and LaNesha Tabb

The Wild Card by Hope and Wade King

Writefully Empowered by Jacob Chastain

The Writing on the Classroom Wall by Steve Wyborney

You Are Poetry by Mike Johnston

You'll Never Guess What I'm Saying by Naomi O'Brien

You'll Never Guess What I'm Thinking About by Naomi O'Brien

INSPIRATION, PROFESSIONAL GROWTH & PERSONAL DEVELOPMENT

Be REAL by Tara Martin

Be the One for Kids by Ryan Sheehy

The Coach ADVenture by Amy Illingworth

Creatively Productive by Lisa Johnson

The Ed Branding Book by Dr. Renae Bryant and Lynette White

Educational Eye Exam by Alicia Ray

The EduNinja Mindset by Jennifer Burdis

Empower Our Girls by Lynmara Colón and Adam Welcome

Finding Lifelines by Andrew Grieve and Andrew Sharos

The Four O'Clock Faculty by Rich Czyz

How Much Water Do We Have? by Pete and Kris Nunweiler

P Is for Pirate by Dave and Shelley Burgess

A Passion for Kindness by Tamara Letter

The Path to Serendipity by Allyson Apsey

PheMOMenal Teacher by Annick Rauch

Recipes for Resilience by Robert A. Martinez

Rogue Leader by Rich Czyz

Sanctuaries by Dan Tricarico

Saving Sycamore by Molly B. Hudgens

The Secret Sauce by Rich Czyz

Shattering the Perfect Teacher Myth by Aaron Hogan

Stories from Webb by Todd Nesloney

Talk to Me by Kim Bearden

Teach Better by Chad Ostrowski, Tiffany Ott, Rae Hughart, and Jeff Gargas

Teach Me, Teacher by Jacob Chastain

Teach, Play, Learn! by Adam Peterson

The Teachers of Oz by Herbie Raad and Nathan Lang-Raad

Teaching Is a Tattoo by Mike Johnston

Teaching the Ms. Abbott Way by Joyce Stephens Abbott

TeamMakers by Laura Robb and Evan Robb

Through the Lens of Serendipity by Allyson Apsey

Write Here and Now by Dan Tricarico

The Zen Teacher by Dan Tricarico

CHILDREN'S BOOKS

The Adventures of Little Mickey by Mickey Smith Jr.

Alpert by LaNesha Tabb

Alpert & Friends by LaNesha Tabb

Beyond Us by Aaron Polansky

Cannonball In by Tara Martin

Dolphins in Trees by Aaron Polansky

Dragon Smart by Tisha and Tommy Richmond

I Can Achieve Anything by MoNique Waters

I Want to Be a Lot by Ashley Savage

The Magic of Wonder by Jenna Copper, Ashley Bible, Abby Gross, and Staci Lamb

Micah's Big Question by Naomi O'Brien

The Princes of Serendip by Allyson Apsey

Ride with Emilio by Richard Nares

A Teacher's Top Secret Confidential by LaNesha Tabb

A Teacher's Top Secret: Mission Accomplished by LaNesha Tabb

The Wild Card Kids by Hope and Wade King

Zom-Be a Design Thinker by Amanda Fox

www.ingramcontent.com/pod-product-compliance
Lightning Source LLC
LaVergne TN
LVHW010659110826
845149LV00014B/3173
9781968898137